*Walt Whitman and
Wallace Stevens*

Walt Whitman and Wallace Stevens

Diane Wood Middlebrook

CORNELL UNIVERSITY PRESS

ITHACA AND LONDON

Acknowledgment is made to Alfred A. Knopf, Inc., and to Faber and Faber Ltd. for permission to quote from the following copyrighted works of Wallace Stevens: *The Necessary Angel, The Collected Poems of Wallace Stevens, Opus Posthumous*, edited by Samuel French Morse, and *Letters of Wallace Stevens*, edited by Holly Stevens.

First published 1974 by Cornell University Press.
Published in the United Kingdom by Cornell University Press Ltd., 2-4 Brook Street, London W1Y 1AA.

International Standard Book Number 0-8014-0832-6
Library of Congress Catalog Card Number 73-20792

Printed in the United States of America by York Composition Co., Inc.

For
  Helen Downey and
  Thomas Isaac Wood

there was always one:

A century in which everything was part
Of that century and of its aspect, a personage,
A man who was the axis of his time,

An image that begot its infantines,
Imaginary poles whose intelligence
Streamed over chaos their civilities.

What is the radial aspect of this place,
This present colony of a colony
Of colonies, a sense in the changing sense

Of things? A figure like Ecclesiast,
Rugged and luminous, chants in the dark
A text that is an answer, although obscure.

—Wallace Stevens,
   "An Ordinary Evening in New Haven"

Acknowledgments

My readings of Whitman and Stevens have profited very much from conversations during graduate study at Yale with Harold Bloom and, later, with my colleagues at Stanford: George Dekker, Kenneth Fields, Albert Gelpi, David Levin, and Herbert Lindenberger. Nina Baym and David Kalstone read the manuscript and wrote indispensable critiques; the editors at Cornell University Press have since provided helpful advice on revision. The Department of English at Stanford University gave me a junior faculty fellowship which relieved me of teaching duties. Stanford also provided substantial grants for secretarial work, which was performed, with my gratitude, by Joan Bowman, Chris Gwynn, Vern McGee, and Rebecca Reynolds. Jonathan Middlebrook, Michole Wood Nicholson, and Zelmira Ruiz were generous in freeing me from other duties during crucial periods in the preparation of this book. Previous critics of Whitman and Stevens, both those quoted and not quoted in these pages, have contributed greatly to my understanding of the poetry and the men, and so have my students at Stanford.

Introductory material and notes by Harold Blodgett and Sculley Bradley are quoted from *Leaves of Grass, Comprehensive Reader's Edition*, with the permission of New York University Press, copyright 1965 by New York University.

DIANE WOOD MIDDLEBROOK

San Francisco, California

Contents

‹

Abbreviations

Letters in parentheses in the text refer to the following books:

LG: Walt Whitman. *Leaves of Grass, Comprehensive Reader's Edition.* Edited and with an introduction by Harold Boldgett and Sculley Bradley. New York: New York University Press, 1965.

CP: The Collected Poems of Wallace Stevens. New York: Alfred A. Knopf, 1954.

LWS: Letters of Wallace Stevens. Edited by Holly Stevens. New York: Alfred A. Knopf, 1967.

NA: Wallace Stevens. *The Necessary Angel: Essays on Reality and the Imagination.* New York: Random House, 1951.

OP: Wallace Stevens. *Opus Posthumous.* Edited and with an introduction by Samuel French Morse. New York: Alfred A. Knopf, 1959.

*Walt Whitman and
Wallace Stevens*

Introduction

The Mythology
of Imagination

One Sunday in February 1955, Wallace Stevens spent several hours reading the poetry of Walt Whitman. Apparently he had been asked by the editor of the *Hudson Review* to comment on Whitman in conjunction with the centennial of the first edition of *Leaves of Grass*. Since his wife had been ill and his own health was failing, Stevens declined to write a formal essay. But he did write a thoughtful letter to the editor of *Hudson* detailing his impressions of Whitman.

I can well believe that he remains highly vital for many people. The poems in which he collects large numbers of concrete things, particularly things each of which is poetic in itself or as part of the collection, have a validity which, for many people, must be enough and must seem to them all opulence and elan.

For others, I imagine that what was once opulent begins to look a little threadbare and the collections seem substitutes for opulence even though they remain gatherings-together of precious Americana, certain to remain precious but not certain to remain poetry. The typical elan survives in many things. . . .

It is useless to treat everything in Whitman as of equal merit. A great deal of it exhibits little or none of his specific power. He seems often to have driven himself to write like himself. The good things, the superbly beautiful and moving things, are those that he wrote naturally, with an extemporaneous and irrepressible vehemence of emotion. [*LWS* 870–871]

Six months later Stevens died: a neat parenthesis of a century encloses these literary careers once and for all. It should be said that though Whitman and Stevens shared a nationality, they shared little else as private citizens; politically, socially, and temperamentally they were too different to measure in terms of one another. As writers, however, they made analogous contributions to American literature and to modern poetry.

Stevens names in his letter two characteristics of Whitman's writing which he admired and sought to achieve in his own: concreteness and elan. Stevens especially valued effects in poetry which convey, as Whitman's catalogues do, " 'the joy of having a body, the voluptuousness of looking' " (CP 136). The catalogue, with its technique of apparently unselective *mentioning*, exists in poetry just this side of silence; the very concreteness of the things named continually beckons the mind out of interpretation into sheer enchanted perception, as Whitman acknowledges: "If you would understand me go to the heights or water-shore, / The nearest gnat is an explanation, and a drop or motion of waves a key" (LG 85). Stevens carries this theme even further. Particularly the poems Stevens wrote late in life express his satisfaction with the way certain objects, being themselves replete with "extraordinary actuality,"[1] defy the poet's designs on them. Writing of a bouquet of roses in sunlight, for example, Stevens says that their crude colors "make any imaginings of them lesser things"

[1] See Stevens' letter to Henry Church (July 2, 1942) on the subject of poets Stevens considers to be the most authoritative spokesmen for the arts in modern (wartime) culture: "the anti-poet may be the right man to discuss EXTRAORDINARY ACTUALITY, and by discussing it in his own way reveal the poetry of the thing" (LWS 411). This idea, refined, reappears in "Adagia": "In the presence of extraordinary actuality, consciousness takes the place of imagination" (OP 165).

(*CP* 430). Paradoxically, their power to silence the rhetorician evokes a feeling so strong the poet is drawn irresistibly to find metaphors expressive of his sense of them; though "sense exceeds all metaphor" the result of this encounter between man and roses is a very good poem in blank verse. "Bouquet of Roses in Sunlight," for all its difference in tone and metaphor, is a thematic twin of "Crossing Brooklyn Ferry," "Song of the Open Road," "There Was a Child Went Forth," and numerous other poems in which Whitman salutes and celebrates the "dumb, beautiful ministers" (*LG* 165) that wait everywhere in common life for the light of sense to fall on them and transform them into meanings.

In his love of concrete objects perceived "with irrepressible vehemence of emotion," however, Stevens is no more like Walt Whitman than are most of the other poets who accompanied Ezra Pound out of the nineteenth century into Imagism, and thence on to the making of long poems. Stevens' resemblance to Whitman lies deeper, in the area of a shared theory of poetry which derives ultimately from Coleridge's concept of the imagination, and was translated into American idioms in the writings of Ralph Waldo Emerson. Briefly summarized, this theory assumes that there are two mental conditions: an ordinary, workaday state of mind and a creative state of mind; when the mind ascends to its creative mode, the man transcends his own ego and can utter universal truths: he becomes a poet. "In a century, in a millennium, one or two men; that is to say, one or two approximations to the right state of every man," writes Emerson. "All the rest behold in the hero or the poet their own green and crude being,—ripened."[2] On the basis of this concept of the poten-

[2] *The Complete Works of Ralph Waldo Emerson*, Centenary edition, ed. and with an introduction by Edward Waldo Emerson, 12 vols. (Boston: Houghton, Mifflin, 1903), I, 106.

tial poet in the ordinary man, Whitman and Stevens formulate what Stevens called "supreme fictions": myths in which the human imagination is personified and given a heroic role in new epics of American culture.

The poetic forms Whitman and Stevens use are quite dissimilar. The form Whitman created resembles Wordsworthian poetic autobiography, but is freer of interpreted recollection. For want of a better generic term, Whitman's poems on the identity of imagination might be called autobiography as myth: particulars are selected to represent the life of the imagination rather than being valued as formative elements in the continuity and meaning of Whitman's personal life. Many of the experiences Whitman the myth-maker assigns to the narrator "I" verifiably did not happen to Whitman the man, but were culled from pictures, books, newspapers, or conversations—or invented. The form Stevens eventually developed was explicitly fictional and scrupulously impersonal. Stevens' poetic hero "I" is autobiographical only insofar as he enacts the instant of perception when an aspect of reality "captives the being, widens—and was there" (*CP* 440). Yet the intentions of Whitman and Stevens were the same: to give a local habitation and the name "I" to the imagination of what Emerson calls the One Man, and to make their poetry the imitation of his mind integrating the worlds of perception, feeling, and action.

In the poems discussed in this book, the momentary confrontation between mind and object becomes the central drama. The psychic processes of imagination in its twofold movement of perception and form-finding are projected as characters, heroes on a quest for meaning. Whitman and Stevens write, in the early *Leaves of Grass* and the late *Collected Poems* respectively, what can best be described as a mythology of imagination. Mythology, because for each poet the heroic "I" was a fictive being, one who magnificently transcended the "malady of the quotidian" (*CP* 96) and fully expressed the poet, but only during rare moments of vision. Mythology of *imagination*, because the very design of this fictive self derives from Coleridgean ideas about the mind, and because in characterizing that self, the poets emphasize the discontinuous nature of imaginative acts. Their heroic chants are rendered, in Whitman's words, "ere all eludes me, hurriedly" (*LG* 247), in the face of death and in the knowledge that the gift of larger being is both temporary and perhaps not recurrent. Their affirmations are limited to the swift instant when the mind reveals its power over the immensity and formlessness of reality and can proclaim

> The meaning of the capture, this hard prize,
> Fully made, fully apparent, fully found. [*CP* 376]

Since the myths of Whitman and Stevens are analogous rather than identical, I discuss the poets separately but symmetrically, treating first the identity of the heroic "I" in each poet's myth, and then the actions attributed to this fictive ego.

My discussion is not based on an idea of influence. *The Collected Poems of Wallace Stevens* shows little trace of Whitman where we might look for him, in Stevens' diction or in his use of the line or in his sense of himself as bardic narrator. Whitman's legacy to Stevens, a gift to claim "at every hazard" (*LG* 29), was not a legacy of poetic style, but a conception of the unfailing sufficiency of the mind's creative relation to reality. But Stevens conveys the essence of his relation to Whitman in a poem where he contemplates his American nativity and his own place in a tradition that begins, in American poetry, with Whitman.

> And tradition is near.
> It joins and does not separate. What, then,
> Is its true form?
>   . . . . .

It has a clear, a single, a solid form,
That of the son who bears upon his back
The father that he loves, and bears him from
The ruins of the past, out of nothing left,
Made noble by the honor he receives,
As if in a golden cloud. The son restores
The father. He hides his ancient blue beneath

His own bright red. But he bears him out of love,
His life made double by his father's life,
Ascending the humane.   [*OP* 86–87]

Chapter 1

Whitman's Supreme Fiction:
The Real Me

> I am an acme of things accomplish'd, and I am
> encloser of things to be.
> —"Song of Myself"

In January 1872, Walt Whitman wrote a letter to Edward Dowden, an English reviewer, thanking him for praising the English edition of *Leaves of Grass:*

I think the main theme you exploit is really of the first importance —and all the rest can be broached & led to, through it, as well as any other way.

I would say that (as you of course see) the spine or verteber principle of my book is a model or ideal (for the service of the New World, & to be gradually absorbed in it) of a complete, healthy, heroic, practical modern *Man.* . . . I seek to typify a living Human Personality, immensely animal, with immense passion, immense amativeness, immense adhesiveness—in the woman immense maternity—& then, in both, immenser far a *moral conscience,* & in always recognizing the direct and indirect control of the divine laws through all and over all forever.[1]

What Whitman singles out as Dowden's main theme is actually a rather minor point in that long and perceptive article,

---

[1] *The Correspondence,* ed. Edwin Haviland Miller, 4 vols. (New York: New York University Press, 1961), II, 154.

which Dowden, significantly, titled "The Poetry of Democracy: Walt Whitman." Dowden's chief concern is to suggest new critical methods and principles of judgment by means of which a "democratic" (American) art—as opposed to an "aristocratic" (European) art—could be rightly understood, and his discussion of Whitman is designed to illustrate the usefulness of the principles he proposes. Whitman's letter suggests, however, that he found two paragraphs of Dowden's essay particularly pertinent. In one paragraph Dowden insists that *Leaves of Grass* is not an obscene book. Whitman abandoned "animality" and "immense passion" as themes worthy of *Leaves of Grass* after 1860, the year the notorious *Calamus* poems appeared. His current, more culturally manageable subjects were "Politics . . . and the pensive thought of Immortality."[2] Yet he continued to believe, accurately, that his best poems concerned intense personal experience. In another passage. Dowden praised Whitman's success in fictionalizing himself: "His own personality as far as he can give it expression or is conscious of it—that identity of himself, which is the hardest of all facts and the only entrance to all facts, is yet no more than the image projected by another ego, the real *Me*."[3]

Here Dowden locates Whitman's most influential achievement in *Leaves of Grass*. Whitman's "Real Me," the "living Human Personality" he describes for Dowden, is a persona elusively autobiographical in origin but Whitman's most important invention. The myth that tells of his life appear in seven poems published in the first three editions of *Leaves of Grass*

[2] "Preface, 1876, to the Centennial Edition," *LG* 746.

[3] Dowden's essay appeared first in the *Westminster Review* for July 1871, and was reprinted in the book from which I quote: Dowden, *Studies in Literature, 1789–1877* (London: K. Paul, Trench, 1877), p. 505.

(1855, 1856, 1860): "There Was a Child Went Forth," "Out of the Cradle Endlessly Rocking," "Starting from Paumanok," "Song of Myself," "The Sleepers," "As I Ebb'd with the Ocean of Life," and "So Long!" In these, Whitman distinguishes between two selves: that of the everyday man, and that of the poet. The myth concerns the emergence of the poet—"the Real Me"—in the man, and his departure from the man. The Real Me is a personification of the act of knowing. His history begins with the child's first consciousness of the world, when he absorbs everything, making few distinctions. "There Was a Child Went Forth" describes that period of awakening perception and introduces into Whitman's myth two crucial assumptions about the relationship of the mind to the world. The first of these is the Romantic principle on which Wordsworth founded *The Prelude*: "exquisitely the individual Mind / . . . to the external World / Is fitted . . . [and] The external World is fitted to the Mind."[4] Reality is naturally intelligible: that is Whitman's first assumption in "A Child Went Forth." His second is that the process which naturally incorporates reality in the mind creates a powerful identity, full of grace, who persists in the man throughout the changing conditions of his life:

> There was a child went forth every day,
> And the first object he look'd upon, that object he became,
> And that object became part of him for the day or a certain
>   part of the day,
> Or for many years or stretching cycles of years
>
>   . . . . .
>
>   became part of that child who went forth every day,
>   and who now goes, and will always go forth every day.
>   [LG 364–366]

---

[4] Wordsworth, "Prospectus" to the 1814 edition of *The Excursion*, lines 63–68.

It is this persisting identity, the rapt perceiver, whom Whitman will single out to capitalize as the Real Me.

"Out of the Cradle Endlessly Rocking" describes the boy's initiation into adolescence as it affects his vocation as a poet. The young child's consciousness as represented in "A Child Went Forth" includes blank misgiving as well as pleasurable curiosity—"the sense of what is real, the thought if after all it should prove unreal" (*LG* 365). In the second poem we watch his ambivalence give way to joyful recognition that the tongue may be used to tell as well as to taste, and experience may be mastered as well as suffered. Specifically this recognition "wakens" the boy to a sense of his identity:

> For I, that was a child, my tongue's use sleeping, now I have
>   heard you,
> Now in a moment I know what I am for, I awake,
> And already a thousand singers, a thousand songs, clearer,
>   louder and more sorrowful than yours,
> A thousand warbling echoes have started to life within me,
>   never to die. [*LG* 251–252]

The third poem in Whitman's fictive autobiography, "Starting from Paumanok," is spoken by the Real Me during late adolescence, on the verge of his maturity. His subjects are the social choices which Erik Erikson has associated with the period of "identity crisis" separating youth from manhood: the choices of a mode of work and of a mode of intimacy. Erikson quotes Freud's terse formula concerning what a normal adult should be able to do well: "Lieben und arbeiten"— love and work. Erikson observes further that the adolescent's preparation for that state of competent maturity chiefly involves the consolidation of the principles upon which he will act. "The adolescent mind," Erikson writes, "is essentially a mind of the *moratorium*, a psychosocial stage between childhood and adulthood, and between the morality learned by the child, and the ethics to be developed by the adult. It is an ideological mind." Erikson summarizes the sense of ego identity consolidated during this stage as "the accrued confidence that the inner sameness and continuity prepared in the past are matched by the sameness and continuity of one's meaning for others, as evidenced in the tangible promise of a 'career.' "[5]

Extending Erikson's generalizations to Whitman's fictive autobiography, we can regard the Real Me in "Starting from Paumanok" as discovering the social meanings of the "clues" to identity he has gathered in "Out of the Cradle Endlessly Rocking." The poet's vocation, of course, involves both a special kind of productivity and a special kind of generative love. Whitman describes the latter as a marriage with "the satisfier, after long-waiting now advancing," who turns out to be "my mistress the soul" (*LG* 18). He pledges himself to the democratic and aesthetic ideologies which shape content and style in *Leaves of Grass* (Sections 6–15). At the end of the poem, with an adolescent's sense of boundless possibility, he launches himself into his profession:

> Expanding and swift, henceforth,
> Elements, breeds, adjustments, turbulent, quick and audacious,
> A world primal again, vistas of glory incessant and branching,
> A new race dominating previous ones and grander far, with
>   new contests,
> New politics, new literatures and religions, new inventions
>   and arts.

> These, my voice announcing—I will sleep no more but arise,
> You oceans that have been calm within me! how I feel you,
>   fathomless, stirring, preparing unprecedented waves and
>   storms.   [*LG* 26–27]

[5] Erikson, *Childhood and Society* (New York: Norton, 1963), pp. 261–265.

The verbs in "Starting from Paumanok" are predominantly future tense. In "Song of Myself," the central poem of Whitman's myth, the verbs are almost exclusively present tense. "Song of Myself" deals with a day in the life of the hero. It records the extensions of his heroic imagination as he confronts and masters for the mind all that is not himself. At the end of the poem he yields into our hands a world that has been searched out to its farthest extensions, high or low, and can no longer be distinguished from himself:

> The last scud of day holds back for me,
> It flings my likeness after the rest and true as any on the
> shadow'd wilds,
>
> .   .   .   .   .
>
> If you want me again look for me under your boot-soles.
>
> [LG 89]

Whitman's fiction of the Real Me is completed in two poems that acknowledge his potential for withdrawal from the living man's mind. "As I Ebb'd with the Ocean of Life" concerns the poet's alienation from his own completed work, incorporating into his myth the essential insight that, to use Wallace Stevens' succinct phrase, the imagination "must change." "So Long!" affirms that recognition, and becomes Whitman's epitaph for the Real Me.

Whitman did not publish these poems in the order listed here; he was not so programmatic in designing his myth as I will be in describing it.[6] Rather, the story of the Real Me be-

---

[6] The poems were published in this order: "Song of Myself," "The Sleepers," and "There Was a Child Went Forth" in the first edition of *Leaves of Grass* (1855); "Out of the Cradle Endlessly Rocking" in the Christmas number (Dec. 24, 1859) of the New York *Saturday Press* under the title "A Child's Reminiscence"; "As I Ebb'd with the Ocean of Life" in *Atlantic Monthly*, April 1860, under the title "Bardic Symbols"; "Starting from Paumanok" and "So Long!" in the

gan, on the opening pages of the first *Leaves of Grass*, with the creation of a fictive hero out of a union between body and soul in the poem finally titled "Song of Myself."

"Song of Myself"

Prior to writing his most ambitious poem, Wallace Stevens claimed that the most influential achievement of art at any period is the creation of an image of man which is both noble and credible. Poems that perform this function for culture he calls "supreme fictions." Eventually he listed for the supreme fiction three qualifications: it must be abstract, it must change, and it must give pleasure.[7] Stevens' formula is applicable to Walt Whitman's best poem. "Song of Myself" is formally and technically unlike *Notes toward a Supreme Fiction*. But it moves through meditation to insight to affirmation, like Stevens' poem, under the influence of these principles.

"Song of Myself" is divided into 52 numbered sections. Sections 1–5 form a preface, while 6–47 contain the action of the poem. Sections 48–52 form its closure. The preface performs for "Song of Myself" what the thirty cantos of "It Must Be Abstract" perform for Stevens' *Notes*. It establishes the identity of "Myself," or "the Real Me," as a fiction—the personification of an act of imagination. The action of the

---

third edition of *Leaves of Grass* (1860)—though Whitman's notebooks indicate that he began composing "Starting from Paumanok" immediately after publishing the first *Leaves of Grass*.

[7] Stevens' statements concerning the necessity for a noble poetry occur chiefly in *The Necessary Angel*, in the essays titled "The Noble Rider and the Sound of Words," "The Figure of the Youth as Virile Poet," and "Imagination as Value." Definitions of the nature of supreme fictions may be found throughout Stevens' letters. See especially his letter to Henry Church, *LWS* 429–432, and the biographical note he encloses in the letter to Eleanor Peters, *LWS* 819–820.

poem (6–47) has four phases and is structured according to the fluctuations of that imagination as it operates in areas of reality which more and more challenge its pleasure-giving capacity for insight and incorporation.

Preface: The Supreme Fiction Must Be Abstract

When Wallace Stevens said that the supreme fiction must be abstract, he meant, among other things, that its hero should be fully an imaginative and allegorical creation, not derived too specifically from biography and not designed too strictly according to an ideology. His would be the voice of a man conceived as standing in "the radiant and productive atmosphere" of his cultural milieu, expressing both his culture's traditions and its contemporary yearning for transformation. His tone would be personal, and his sensibility abstracted from the poet's own individual tastes and susceptibilities. But he would not be merely a projection of the poet's ego.[8] "Give him no names," Stevens cautions himself in the first part of *Notes;* "look not at his colored eyes. . . . / The hot of him is purest in the heart" (*CP* 388). Only at the very end of the poem, after much preparation, Stevens reveals the name of "major man" to be "I" (*CP* 404–406).

Stevens' anchoring of the hero in the subjective personal pronoun, however, remains a conscious rhetorical strategy. Most characteristically his hero is humane but distant, a

contrivance of the spectre of the spheres,

> Contriving balance to contrive a whole,
> The vital, the never-failing genius,
> Fulfilling his meditations, great and small.
> ["The Auroras of Autumn," *CP* 420]

[8] These statements are abstracted and condensed from "The Figure of the Youth as Virile Poet," *NA* 39–67.

"The Real Me," on the other hand, is a biographical personality, "solid and sound," from the opening syllable of his poem:

> I celebrate myself, and sing myself,
> And what I assume you shall assume,
> For every atom belonging to me as good belongs to you.
>
> I loafe and invite my soul,
> I lean and loafe at my ease observing a spear of summer grass.
>
> My tongue, every atom of my blood, form'd from this soil,
>   this air,
> Born here of parents born here from parents the same, and
>   their parents the same,
> I, now thirty-seven years old in perfect health begin,
> Hoping to cease not till death.   [LG 28–29]

I quote from the poetry at length here to acknowledge at once, in this discussion of the "fictive" or "abstract" nature of Stevens' and Whitman's heroic personae, the crucial differences in their temperaments and in their approaches to the materials of the heroic poem. "The Auroras of Autumn" represents Stevens in his full maturity, and it is one of his most personal poems: nostalgic, nightmare-haunted, valedictory. Stevens is greatly at ease with his subject, and he is equally at ease with the blank-verse line which, loosened by many anapests, has become the characteristic medium for his meditations. Relaxed as the mood and the line structure are, however, "The Auroras of Autumn" conveys a profound formality—especially when juxtaposed with the free rhythms and insistent personalism of Whitman's "Song of Myself." The contrived "never-failing genius, / Fulfilling his meditations" in "Auroras" is a "philosophers' man" (CP 250); "the Real Me" is native to the body of Walt Whitman—"The feeling of health, the full-noon trill, the song of me rising from bed and meeting the sun" (*LG* 30). Nonetheless, the two poets are comparable in their orientations and achievements as myth-makers. Functioning within the myths of the heroic self that each poet explores is a similar set of beliefs about the mind, the source of which is ultimately, though indirectly, Coler-idge's theory of imagination. It is at this level of abstraction that I wish to compare them.

Since Coleridge's most illuminating remarks about imagina-tion occur as digressions scattered throughout his writings, the critic who wishes to make use of them picks and chooses texts according to his interpretation of what Coleridge meant.[9] For the purposes of this study I wish to single out two fundamen-tal ideas.

The first of these is that imagination is not one particular organ or faculty of perception. Rather, it is an uncustomary condition of human being, one wherein the organs of sense and the mental faculties combine their powers to produce a state of acute, creative awareness. Coleridge asserts in *The Statesman's Manual* that during the state of imaginative per-ception the reason and the data of the senses are "reconciled"; imagination is "that reconciling and mediatory power which *incorporating* the reason in images of the sense and organiz-ing the . . . flux of the senses by the permanence and self-circling energies of the reason, gives birth to a system of sym-

[9] My understanding of Coleridge is indebted to the introduction and notes in the two-volume edition of *Biographia Literaria* pre-pared by John Shawcross (London: Clarendon Press, 1907) and to Walter Jackson Bate's excellent critical biography, *Coleridge* (New York: Macmillan, 1968). It differs significantly from the reading of Coleridge which forms the basis of Frank Lentricchia's judgment that Wallace Stevens "was not a Coleridgean"; see *The Gaiety of Lan-guage* (Berkeley: University of California Press, 1968), especially pages 119–127.

bols, harmonious in themselves, and consubstantial with the truths of which they are the conductors."[10]

The emphasis on "incorporating" here is mine. One of Coleridge's most influential insights is that truth must be conducted into "images of the sense" before it can have significance. Coleridge emphasizes this point in his essay "On Poesy or Art," where he describes the "universals" discovered by the discursive understanding as being "without character, as water is purest when without taste, smell or color."[11] Art makes truth accessible; truth is inhuman until it has been "completed" by reception into the particular sensibility of a living man: "Of the discursive understanding, which forms for itself general notions of classification for the purpose of comparing and arranging *phenomena*, the characteristic is clearness without depth. . . . The completing power which unites clearness with depth, the plenitude of the sense with the comprehensibility of the understanding, is the imagination, impregnated with which the understanding itself becomes intuitive, and a living power."[12] Lacking the active presence of imagination to complete the mind, intellect detaches from feeling, alienating the mind from the things it beholds. Objects go back to being "fixed and dead,"[13] and the man feels less than himself:

> My genial spirits fail;
> And what can these avail
> To lift the smothering weight from off my breast?

[10] *The Complete Works of Samuel Taylor Coleridge*, ed. W. G. T. Shedd, 7 vols. (New York: Harper & Brothers, 1889), I, 436.

[11] Coleridge, *Biographia Literaria*, ed. Shawcross, II, 262.

[12] See "Appendix B," *The Statesman's Manual*, in *Complete Works*, ed. Shedd, I, 460–461.

[13] "All objects (*as* objects) are essentially fixed and dead," *Biographia Literaria*, ed. Shawcross, I, 202.

It were a vain endeavor,
Though I should gaze for ever
On that green light that lingers in the west:
I may not hope from outward forms to win
The passion and the life, whose fountains are within.

["Dejection: An Ode"]

"Imagination" is Coleridge's term for the power which allows an individual mind to attain a state of integration involving all resources of feeling and thought. Since it is a power—as opposed to an intellectual faculty or organ of sense—its nature is active and temporal. And this brings me to the second of Coleridge's ideas about imagination I want to isolate here: his understanding of the structure of the act of imagination. Coleridge distinguished two different phases: a phase of abstraction and a phase of symbol-making. The imagination, in converting truth into significance, "connects the active with the passive powers of our nature, the intellect with the senses; and its appointed function is to elevate the *images* of the latter, while it realizes the *ideas* of the former."[14] This same concept is the substance of the famous definition of imagination in *Biographia Literaria* where Coleridge identifies these phases as "primary" and "secondary":

The IMAGINATION then, I consider as either primary, or secondary. The primary IMAGINATION I hold to be the living Power and prime Agent of all human perception, and as a repetition in the finite mind of the eternal act of creation in the infinite I AM. The secondary Imagination I consider as an echo of the former, co-existing with the conscious will, yet still identical with the primary in the *kind* of its agency, and differing only in *degree*, and in the *mode* of its operation. It dissolves,

[14] "On the Principles of Genial Criticism," *Biographia Literaria*, ed. Shawcross, II, 227.

diffuses, dissipates, in order to re-create; or where this process is rendered impossible, yet still at all events it struggles to idealize and to unify. It is essentially *vital*, even as all objects (*as* objects) are essentially fixed and dead.[15]

Coleridge adds elsewhere that the perceptiveness he describes as the primary phase is not the same thing as mere observation of phenomena. Rather, it is "an inward beholding, having a similar relation to the intelligible or spiritual, as Sense has to the material or phenomenal."[16] He elaborates this thesis in the essay "On Poesy or Art." Quarreling politely with the definition of art as an imitation of nature, Coleridge observes that the primary act of imagination involves *withdrawal* from nature, into the personal I AM, where abstraction precedes image:

The artist must first eloign himself from nature in order to return to her with full effect. Why this? Because if he were to begin by mere painful copying, he would produce masks only, not forms breathing life. He must out of his own mind create forms according to the severe laws of the intellect, in order to generate in himself that co-ordination of freedom and law, that involution of obedience in the prescript, and of the prescript in the impulse to obey, which assimilates him to nature, and enables him to understand her. He merely absents himself a season from her, that his own spirit, which has the same ground with nature, may learn her unspoken language in its main radicals, before he approaches to her endless composition of them.[17]

The secondary act of imagination succeeds the primary, integrating the universal with the particular, law with form. It

[15] *Biographia Literaria*, ed. Shawcross, I, 202.
[16] Coleridge, "Aids to Reflection," *Complete Works*, ed. Shedd, I, 256.
[17] Coleridge, "On Poesy or Art," *Biographia Literaria*, ed. Shawcross, II, 258.

has been described by Coleridge's commentator John Shawcross as "a more highly potentialized form of the primary";
for while imagination "in its primary form unconsciously
draws all experience into relation with the self," in its secondary form, with the aid of conscious will, it "reflects that
self more perfectly in an ideal world."[18]
Finally, Coleridge considers the livingness of the "living
power of imagination" to be its power of *movement* between
image and abstraction. The vital principle in nature which
produces seasons of growth and decay and the boundless pro-
liferation of organic forms has its mental counterpart in what
Coleridge describes as "the permanent and self-circling energies of the reason." The regenerated mind endlessly cycles between its two poles, abstraction and form, in a process of
composition that, by analogy with nature, might ideally be
regarded as endless.

Coleridge's thinking about the imagination generated few
poems, except in the heads of other poets, but it enabled him
in *Biographia Literaria* to argue influentially for the tough
reasonableness beneath Wordsworth's artifice of simplicity.
His theory as summarized above has the same usefulness with
reference to Whitman and to Stevens. Coleridge's theory of
imagination did not inspire "Song of Myself" or *Notes toward a Supreme Fiction* as it inspired *The Prelude*—though
Whitman spoke enthusiastically of *Biographia Literaria* in the
period of eclectic reading which preceded publication of the
first *Leaves of Grass.*[19] Coleridge's usefulness is that he articulates the ideology discoverable within the body of "Song of

---

[18] *Biographia Literaria*, ed. Shawcross, I, IXXV. Italics mine.
[19] Roger Asselineau points out that Whitman reviewed *Biographia
Literaria* for the *Brooklyn Eagle* on Dec. 4, 1847; see his *The Evolution of Walt Whitman*, 2 vols. (Cambridge: The Belknap Press, 1962),
II, 40, 287.

Myself." These ideas were obviously not held consciously by Whitman as he was writing: like Stevens, Whitman apparently avoided holding too many ideas while writing poems. "Say what you will," Stevens once told a critic. "But we are dealing with poetry, not with philosophy. The last thing in the world that I should want to do would be to formulate a system" (*LWS* 864). Nonetheless, as Whitman's poem takes shape it forms ideas comparable to the ideas that shape the action of *Notes toward a Supreme Fiction*, and those ideas deeply inform what I am identifying as its preface.

Sections 1–5

In the preface to "Song of Myself," Whitman is solely concerned with making distinctions between his ordinary self and the persona he described to Dowden as "a model or ideal . . . modern *Man*," the Real Me. Both selves are present in this section, standing in the relation to each other of subject and object—as indicated in the first line of the poem:

I celebrate myself, and sing myself.

"I" is the consciousness of the poet. "Myself" is an ideal abstracted from the poet's ego. At section 5 they are made one; "Myself" subsumes "I" and becomes the speaker of the poem.

"Song of Myself" opens on the image of a man taking his ease: leaning on something, "loafing," looking at the grass. Whitman's preface to the first edition announces that his intention in *Leaves of Grass* is epic and heroic; probably no other epic opens with so little pomp. Yet the great theme of "Song of Myself," Imagination, has been engaged at the moment when the loafer's eye alights on an object of perception:

I loafe and invite my soul,
I lean and loafe at my ease observing a spear of summer grass.

[*LG* 28]

The spear of summer grass, subjugated by the imagination in this first movement of the poem's action, will become the chief metaphor for reality in "Song of Myself" and furnish Whitman's book its title through every edition. At this point, however, it is merely an object, for Whitman is here describing himself in a condition of unimaginativeness, unready to write "Song of Myself" just yet. He is waiting for something and killing time with a little talk about himself (sections 2–4). What he awaits is a completing of intelligence with reference to his subject, a completion that cannot be achieved through traditional interpretations of reality as formalized by "creeds and schools." He awaits the moment when the undifferentiated hum of the soul's "valvèd voice" will grow articulate in the throat of the living Me.

This image of the loafing poet is central to the Romantic ideology of the poem. It has a charming parallel in "Frost at Midnight," where Coleridge describes himself as taking a little time off from reading abstruse philosophy. As he listens to the silence of the night and lovingly watches his sleeping son, the world begins to compose itself around him. The abstractions which had been tiring his head begin to come alive in particulars, and the poem moves to closure affirming the profound intelligibility of things. "Therefore all seasons shall be sweet to thee," he concludes.

Whether the summer clothe the general earth
With greenness, or the redbreast sit and sing
Between the tufts of snow on the bare branch
Of mossy apple-tree, while the nigh thatch
Smokes in the sun-thaw; whether the eave-drops fall

Heard only in the trances of the blast,
Or if the secret ministry of frost
Shall hang them up in silent icicles,
Quietly shining to the quiet Moon.

An even more illuminating parallel may be located in a key
passage of Stevens' "It Must Be Abstract," where Stevens
specifically contrasts two states of perception, imaginative and
unimaginative:

The first idea is an imagined thing.

. . . . .

If MacCullough himself lay lounging by the sea,

Drowned in its washes, reading in the sound,
About the thinker of the first idea,
He might take habit, whether from wave or phrase,

Or power of the wave, or deepened speech,
Or a leaner being, moving in on him,
Of greater aptitude and apprehension,

As if the waves at last were never broken,
As if the language suddenly, with ease,
Said things it had laboriously spoken.   [CP 387]

In Stevens, as in Whitman, the figure on whom imagination
descends is characteristically a lounger—prone, or otherwise
at his ease in a sensuous setting. If not specifically reading a
book, this figure is "reading" as "MacCullough" reads, drawing from text or memory some specific large idea which suddenly enlivens the particulars of his surroundings. Like the
English Romantic poets, Stevens associates the pleasure this
experience gives his "scholar" with the feelings of a lover for
his mistress (see "Final Soliloquy of the Interior Paramour")
or a husband for his wife (see "It Must Give Pleasure" CP
406). But the event itself is usually not portrayed in sexual

metaphors. In Whitman, however, sexual excitement is a matrix of metaphor for terms describing the relation between imagination and reality. The Real Me, "caresser of life" (*LG* 40), is created at the instant when the senses are possessed by the spirit of intelligibility. This occurs in "Song of Myself" at section 5, where the soul, invited in section 1, finally arrives and releases the poet from idleness into song:

> I believe in you my soul, the other I am must not abase itself
> to you,
> And you must not be abased to the other.
>
> Loafe with me on the grass, loose the stop from your throat,
> Not words, not music or rhyme I want, not custom or lecture,
> not even the best,
> Only the lull I like, the hum of your valvèd voice.
>
> I mind how once we lay such a transparent summer morning,
> How you settled your head athwart my hips and gently
> turn'd over upon me,
> And parted the shirt from my bosom-bone, and plunged your
> tongue to my bare-stript heart,
> And reach'd till you felt my beard, and reach'd till you held
> my feet.
>
> Swiftly arose and spread around me the peace and knowledge
> that pass all the argument of the earth,
> And I know that the hand of God is the promise of my own,
> And I know that the spirit of God is the brother of my own,
> And that all the men ever born are also my brothers, and the
> women my sisters and lovers,
> And that a kelson of the creation is love,
> And limitless are leaves stiff or drooping in the fields,
> And brown ants in the little wells beneath them,
> And mossy scabs of the worm fence, heap'd stones, elder,
> mullein and poke-weed. [*LG* 33]

The explicitly sexual union of soul with body must strike every reader as odd upon first encounter. But the way has been prepared throughout the preceding sections, where Whitman proposes (though by indirection) a theory of imagination which rests on an analogy between human creativity and the "procreant urge" of Nature. These sections demonstrate that "contact" is "the origin of all poems" (section 2).

The creation of poetry involves two kinds of contact, the contact of soul with body (understanding with sensation), and the contact of Me with Not-Me. Whitman explores these alternately in sections 2 and 3. These sections perform two functions which prepare for the descent of the soul in section 5. First, they establish "soul" as the "procreant urge" operating in all of nature to produce form: "Always a knit of identity, always distinction, always a breed of life" (*LG* 31). In nonhuman nature, soul insures the continuing presence of substance; manifested as the sex instinct it keeps creation in existence.

> Urge and urge and urge,
> Always the procreant urge of the world.

> Out of the dimness opposite equals advance, always substance
> and increase, always sex.   [*LG* 31]

Operating through human nature, soul is the desire for organization and significance. In the words of the Real Me at section 3:

> Clear and sweet is my soul, and clear and sweet is all that is
> not my soul.

> Lack one lacks both, and the unseen is proved by the seen,
> Till that becomes unseen and receives proof in its turn.
> [*LG* 31]

And just as merely "natural" sexual contact requires a condition of undress, so does the contact between mind and matter require that the Real Me become, in a special sense, "undisguised and naked." The ceremony of undressing occurs twice in these opening sections. In the first instance, section 2, the poet feels threatened by the power of aromatic distillations to "intoxicate" him physically, causing one kind of sensation to be dominant. He flees from enclosed to open space, where all five senses spring to life, aroused by contact with mere "atmosphere": air, light, and shade—motions without form. The other occurs at section 3, when he is threatened by the power of abstractions, distilled thought, to distract him from a productive state of mind:

> Showing the best and dividing it from the worst age vexes age,
> Knowing the perfect fitness and equanimity of things, while they discuss I am silent, and go bathe and admire myself.
>
> [*LG* 31]

The gesture of undressing may be regarded as Whitman's characteristic rendering of what Coleridge describes as one mode of the secondary imagination, which "dissolves, diffuses, dissipates, in order to re-create." In this mode, the secondary imagination refuses pre-established forms in order to recover essences. And as the form-dissolving phase of secondary imagination is a kind of preparation for the primary phase, so is divesting the mind preparation for contact with reality, an action usually represented in sexual images.

In his recent study of Whitman, Edwin Haviland Miller discusses at length the sexual basis of the rhythms and the imagery of the early poetry, noting the prevalence of images involving ingestion and gestation. These he attributes to psychic immaturity; "Because he is not afraid to accept and love his own body, he can love the world. . . . But, it must be noted, the eroticism unconsciously reverts to the mother-child relationship, and the verbal aggression is not matched by the protagonist's acts; even in fantasy Whitman cannot easily assume the role of the aggressor."[20]

Miller categorizes Whitman's imagery as "regressive," but if we shift our eyes from psychoanalytic theory to literary history we may observe how pervasively such imagery appears in nineteenth-century poetry unencumbered by the cultural embarrassment Miller's term connotes. As Lionel Trilling has observed with reference to John Keats, much of the richness and subtlety of Keats's art derives from his ability to associate pleasures with one another without thinking of them as "high" or "low." There was a continuum for Keats between the infantile experience of sensual satisfaction and the abstract conceptions of truth and beauty which became the chief preoccupations of his mature mind. Further, as Trilling points out, Keats considered his ability to enjoy sensuous passivity an important resource for his poetry, a capacity analogous to a woman's capacity for sexual pleasure, both in its quality as experience and in its implications. "It is not the least remarkable thing about Keats," says Trilling, that "he had an awareness, rare in our culture, of the female principle as a power, an energy. He does not shrink from experiencing its manifestation in himself, believing it to be half of his power of creation. Yet bold as he is in this, he must still assert the virtue of the specifically 'masculine' energy: even the thrush assures him that 'he's awake who thinks himself asleep,' that by being conscious of his surrender to the passive, unconscious life he has affirmed the active principle."[21]

[20] Miller, *Walt Whitman's Poetry: A Psychological Journey*, p. 97.
[21] Trilling, ed., *The Selected Letters of John Keats* (New York: Farrar, Straus, and Young, 1951), pp. 22–23.

Trilling's remarks apply to Whitman's conception of the Real Me in "Song of Myself." Just as Nature is imaged as coupled energies—ebb and flow, rise and set, merge and outlet—so is the hero's mind conceived as an "electric" combination of male and female susceptibilities. During its primary mode of contact, the mode of perception, it is receptive, incorporative, fertile; the imagination absorbs and gestates. This sense of the female character of primary imagination lies behind the strange and beautiful figure which ends section 3:

> I am satisfied—I see, dance, laugh, sing;
> As the hugging and loving bed-fellow sleeps at my side
>   through the night, and withdraws at the peep of the day
>   with stealthy tread,
> Leaving me baskets cover'd with white towels swelling the
>   house with their plenty,
> Shall I postpone my acceptation and realization . . . ?
>
> [*LG* 31]

In the first edition of *Leaves of Grass,* Whitman identified the loving bedfellow as God. The bulging baskets he leaves suggest both a pregnant belly and the daily bread which, set to rise overnight, becomes the common nourisher of the household by day. These are material analogues to the poems of Myself: "This is the meal equally set, this the meat for natural hunger" (section 19). Out of such amorous contact of the self with the world, when the mind lies all joyfully open to the life around it, will issue the poems of the Real Me throughout the whole length of his song.

The primary imagination is the poet's receptive half, then: "acceptation" precedes "realization" in the creative process. During its secondary, or form-finding, mode the imagination is active, aggressive, intrusive, penetrating. It uncovers, or alternatively, discovers.

Undrape! You are not guilty to me, nor stale nor discarded,
I see through the broadcloth and gingham whether or no,
And am around, tenacious, acquisitive, tireless, and cannot be
    shaken away.   [*LG 35*]

These lines are from section 7, for the secondary mode of
imagination is not released into action until union with the
soul occurs in section 5. But we get a glimpse of it as virile
potential in section 3, where the poet stands, powerfully at
ease, side by side with "this mystery"—presumably the subjects he will penetrate in the course of the poem.

To elaborate is no avail, learn'd and unlearn'd feel that it is so.

Sure as the most certain sure, plumb in the uprights, well
    entretied, braced in the beams,
Stout as a horse, affectionate, haughty, electrical,
I and this mystery here we stand.   [*LG 31*]

I have been speaking of Whitman's concept of soul as the
vital principle both in nature and in the mind which makes
fruitful contact possible. Viewed as a moving force or energy,
soul is the will to form. But it is also a superior condition of
human existence which the man himself only occasionally
possesses. Earlier I referred to that personified energy as "the
spirit of intelligibility"; and I think that is as close as one may
come to a general descriptive term. For Whitman, at this
time, "soul" was a word for the authoritative sympathy which
he sometimes felt, and he apparently could not conceive of
"soul" without incorporating it in a human form resembling
his own. "I cannot understand the mystery," Whitman wrote
in the notebook where the first *Leaves of Grass* was taking
shape, "but I am always conscious of myself as two—as my
soul and I."[22] This self-extension appears as an affectionate

---

[22] MS Notebook I, the earliest extant, reproduced in *The Uncol-
lected Poetry and Prose of Walt Whitman*, ed. Emory Holloway
(Garden City: Doubleday, 1921), II, 66.

companion throughout "Song of Myself" and other poems of
the period 1855–1860:

> Was somebody asking to see the soul?
> See, your own shape and countenance. . . .
>
>   ["Starting from Paumanok"]
>
> Now on this spot I stand with my robust soul.
>
>   ["Song of Myself"]
>
> The soul is always beautiful, it appears more, it appears less,
>   it comes or it lags behind,
> It comes from its embower'd garden and looks pleasantly on
>   itself and encloses the world.   ["The Sleepers"]

Whitman's comfortable tone with reference to the soul
seems to derive from observing its dependence on the body.
Whitman is said to have taken his idea of the soul from Emerson. But the first poems Whitman wrote always emphasize
a detail Emerson dismisses from importance: the body is the
soul's *medium*. Emerson tends to belittle the physical man,
"the eating, drinking, planting, counting man," claiming,
"Him we do not respect[;] but the soul, whose organ he is
would he let it appear through his action, would make our
knees bend."[23] And though Emerson takes a tolerant view of
the enhancement of sensation which extraordinary men such
as poets occasionally allow themselves, he nonetheless makes
a careful distinction between extreme conditions of sense and
extreme conditions of soul: "If in any manner we can stimu-
late this [spiritual] instinct new passages are opened for us
into nature; the mind flows into and through things hardest
and highest, and . . . metamorphosis is possible. This is the
reason why bards love wine, mead, narcotics, coffee, tea,
opium, the fumes of sandalwood and tobacco . . . which are
several coarser or finer *quasi*-mechanical substitutes for the

---

[23] Emerson, *Works*, II, 273.

true nectar, which is the ravishment of the intellect by coming nearer to the fact."[24] At various periods of his life Whitman shared Emerson's suspicion of stimulants and of heightened sensation. But in the poems of the period I am treating here, Whitman consistently associates sexual arousal with the active presence of imagination. In an effort to give metaphysical legitimacy to this idea Whitman in "Song of the Open Road" (1856) goes so far as to attribute to the soul a "fluid and attaching character" analogous to the body's sexual secretions, and occurring with them:

> The efflux of the soul is happiness, here is happiness,
> I think it pervades the open air, waiting at all times,
> Now it flows unto us, we are rightly charged.
>
> . . . . .
>
> Toward the fluid and attaching character exudes the sweat of
>   the love of young and old,
> From it falls distill'd the charm that mocks beauty and attainments,
> Toward it heaves the shuddering longing ache of contact.
>   [LG 153–154]

But for the most part Whitman is content to take for granted that mature sexuality is fundamental to the poet's authority. There are numerous examples of the analogy between carnal and spiritual knowing in the first three editions of *Leaves of Grass*, most notably in the *Calamus* section. And the idea operates significantly in the myth of the Real Me, in the poems treating of his making—"Out of the Cradle Endlessly Rocking,"—and his unmaking—"As I Ebb'd with the Ocean of Life." "Out of the Cradle" portrays the boy's discovery of his poetic vocation following a dramatic recognition of the meaning of the sexual love between two birds. Whitman indi-

---

[24] *Works*, III, 27–28.

cates that the boy's voyeuristic fascination with the mating birds furnishes him both a sexual and spiritual education. "In a moment I know what I am for," the boy cries at the poem's climax, with that line accepting his sexuality and his mortality, as well as what is to be his work as a man. In "As I Ebb'd" Whitman returns to this setting—the beach at Paumanok—to treat an identity crisis of the Real Me. There he describes himself as out of touch (*LG* 254) with the poet in himself; trying to recover the lost identity, he flings himself on the shore as on the breast of another man:

> I throw myself upon your breast my father,
> I cling to you so that you cannot unloose me,
> I hold you so firm till you answer me something.
>
> Kiss me my father,
> Touch me with your lips as I touch those I love,
> Breathe to me while I hold you close the secret of the mur-
>   muring I envy.   [*LG* 255]

This image, elusively both father and lover, is an interesting symbol in Whitman's life as well; after disappearing as the Real Me of the poetry, around 1860, he became the image Whitman projected in letters to young male friends. In letters the sexual love is sublimated—or nearly so—into protective fatherly concern. In the poems, however, sexual desire is admitted to be an important resource of the imagination.

And this brings me, at last, back to "Song of Myself." When the soul finds access to the natural world it must do so through the body, and on the body's terms. Hence its approach to the poet in section 5, to confirm his authority and bestow the power to write the poem, is described in terms implying orgasm:

> you settled your head athwart my hips and gently
>   turn'd over upon me,

> And parted the shirt from my bosom-bone, and plunged your tongue to my bare-stript heart,
> And reach'd till you felt my beard, and reach'd till you held my feet.

> Swiftly arose and spread around me the peace and knowledge that pass all the argument of the earth.   [LG 33]

Like Coleridge's Imagination, Whitman's Soul has the function of consolidating the human powers of intelligence and feeling. Its presence gives the heart a tongue; to return to Coleridge's terms, the soul "unites the plenitude of sense with the understanding," producing a state of peaceful certainty that "the hand of God is the promise of my own" (LG 33).

At this point in "Song of Myself" the prefatory portrait of the Real Me is complete. We know who he is: the authoritative "witness" of reality (section 4). And we know who he is not: the mind blurred by habit, ill-health, or the distractions of common life; the mind dominated by ungenerous feelings, or engrossed by social or intellectual contention:

> People I meet, the effect upon me of my early life or the ward and city I live in, or the nation,
> The latest dates, discoveries, inventions, societies, authors old and new,
> My dinner, dress, associates, looks, compliments, dues,
> The real or fancied indifference of some man or woman I love
>
> .   .   .   .   .
>
> These come to me days and nights and go from me again,
> But they are not the Me myself.   [LG 32]

Viewed from the perspective of Coleridge's categories, the Real Me may be described as a symbol: the personification of imagination in its primary and secondary operation; not a real man, but the projection of a temporary and vulnerable state of mind. However, it is only fair to Whitman to observe that he did not view himself from Coleridge's perspective. Whitman regarded the emergence of this resource, imagination, with joy and awe, and we must believe him when he tells us that he could not have learned merely from reading books to tap its energies. Moreover, the processes by which his poetry was created remained a subject he had no desire to investigate categorically: "while they discuss I am silent, and go bathe and admire myself" (LG 31). But it does not diminish the poem's stature to say that Whitman's mind, like Wordsworth's, taught itself epistemology and metaphysics by studying its own creative sympathies, and conveyed its knowledge in the poetic form of exalted pedagogical autobiography.

The Action: It Must Give Pleasure

"Song of Myself" has epic scope and intention, and its action involves alternating periods of contention and luxuriation. As with other epics, contentions dominate the poem, furnishing climaxes in the action and validating the poet's mood of celebration. In Whitman's epic the contenders are, on the one hand, the Real Me, and on the other, the Not-Me threatening ambush.

Two premises underlie the action of "Song of Myself." One is that the imagination has the power to incorporate whatever lies around it. Its subjects range from the smallest natural objects to abstract conceptions of Man, from spears of grass to sensual appetite and human mortality. The other premise is that the transformation of experience into verbal meanings, which imagination performs, is the most significant of human acts—basis of the poet's claim near the end of the poem that

nothing, not God, is greater to one than one's self is.

[LG 86]

The action of the poem dramatizes the education of the protagonist to the large resources of his own imagination. It begins in section 6 and evolves through four distinguishable phases corresponding to significant shifts in the Real Me's sense of his subject matter and his audience. The phases are not formally distinguished from one another by titles, chapter headings, or even by section numbers—one flows into another. I shall focus on the moments in each phase when a crisis in the identity of the Real Me occurs.

Because the poem is long and digressive, let me briefly summarize here what I take to be the significant development in each phase of its action. The first phase (sections 6–19) is virtually a casebook of demonstrations of Coleridge's idea about the imagination, that it is "the power of humanizing nature, of infusing the thoughts and passions of man into every thing which is the object of contemplation."[25] These sections establish that the imagination's power of incorporation is "limitless [as] leaves" (*LG* 33). The second phase (sections 20–30) begins to test that assumption. The Real Me takes up a subject for poetry which demands the most honest "acceptation" (*LG* 31): his own sexuality. He is tempted into the error, fatal to imagination as conceived in "Song of Myself," of rejecting an aspect of his own body (see section 28: "You villain touch! what are you doing?"). Acknowledging his error, the Real Me recovers his creative energy, only to have it diminished again, in the third phase of the action (sections 31–38), by another seizure of powerful feeling. The source of the first crisis had been an irrational aspect of his own nature; the source of the second is the mimetic power of art. The Real Me is silenced as the actual man succumbs to the vividness of his own images:

[25] "On Poesy or Art," *Biographia Literaria,* ed. Shawcross, II, 253.

> Somehow I have been stunn'd. Stand back!
> Give me a little time beyond my cuff'd head, slumbers,
>   dreams, gaping,
> I discover myself on the verge of a usual mistake.   [*LG* 72]

Instructed by these two threats to his identity the Real Me by the final phase of the action (sections 39–47) has consolidated his powers. What he can impart to other men and women is certainty of the mind's access to universals, the reduction of "multeity into unity":

> Through me the   afflatus surging and surging, through me
>   the current and index.   [*LG* 52]

This is the knowledge that, as Stevens says, "pulls tight the final ring" (*CP* 442), uniting the Real Me with all men. He becomes at last the power of articulation in every human mind, bestowing the forms that "cannot fail" (*LG* 79).

Sections 6–19

In this first phase of the action the Real Me is concerned with testing the intuition which the soul has brought to the man in section 5, that the subjects for poetry are "limitless as leaves." Once the "eyesight behind the eyesight"[26] which the soul adds to sense has opened on the spear of summer grass, that object begins to burgeon into symbols on the speaker's tongue—fourteen of them, more or less, the content of section 6. And then that eye moves upward and outward in the sections through 19, through sweeps of catalogues drawing ever more subjects into the imagination's perspective. The subjects

[26] Whitman's phrase for this phenomenon in his preface to the first edition of *Leaves of Grass:* "From the eyesight proceeds another eyesight and from the hearing proceeds another hearing and from the voice proceeds another voice eternally curious of the harmony of things with man" (*LG* 715).

are diverse, but they have one common characteristic: they, like the grass, are objects sheerly external to the speaker, rather than being subjective states of thought and feeling. His relationship to them is a rhythmic grasping, scrutinizing, and releasing, a process which the speaker summarizes over and over in a kind of refrain that recurs at periodic intervals throughout 6–19:

> I mind them or the show or reasonance of them—I come and
>   I depart.   [*LG* 36]

> In me the caresser of life wherever moving, backward as well
>   as forward sluing,
> To niches aside and junior bending, not a person or object
>   missing,
> Absorbing all to myself and for this song.   [*LG* 40]

> Me going in for my chances, spending for vast returns.
>   [*LG* 41]

> And these tend inward to me, and I tend outward to them,
> And such as it is to be of these more or less I am,
> And of these one and all I weave the song of myself.
>   [*LG* 44]

During this phase of the action the degree of contention between Myself and reality is minimal; the objects he scrutinizes do not interact with him, even to notice him. This phase represents what Wordsworth called "the soul's seed-time," when it is discovering, testing, and developing its powers of incorporation and reconciliation. External objects challenge the Real Me only by sheer diversity and weight of numbers.

Nonetheless, these sections advance the poem's action. They offer demonstrations of the processes by means of which imagination causes reality to yield to the human desire for meaning. I turn again to Stevens, whose principle "It Must Give Pleasure" I take to be as influential in Whitman's poem as in Stevens' own, to recall the speculation that lies near the end of *Notes toward a Supreme Fiction:*

> These things at least comprise
> An occupation, an exercise, a work,
> A thing final in itself and, therefore, good:
>
>   . . . . .
>
> And we enjoy like men, the way a leaf
> Above the table spins its constant spin,
> So that we look at it with pleasure, look
>
> At it spinning its eccentric measure. Perhaps,
> The man-hero is not the exceptional monster,
> But he that of repetition is most master.   [CP 405]

The power of imagination over reality, which Stevens here is bold to call heroic, is its capacity never to see the same thing twice the same way: to produce "the strongest impression of novelty, while it rescues the most admitted truths from the impotence caused by the very circumstances of their universal admission" (Coleridge, *Biographia Literaria,* IV). Its resources are metaphor culled both from abstract "truths" and from purely personal sensibility. For a mature human being these resources exist from instant to instant in combinations that can reasonably be regarded as "limitless." Hence for Stevens as for Whitman the power to enjoy like a man is the power to appropriate for human use the smallest particulars around oneself—a leaf above the table, a spear of summer grass.

Section 6 of "Song of Myself" offers an extensive demonstration of this principle:

A child said *What is the grass?* fetching it to me with full
hands;
How could I answer the child? I do not know what it is any
more than he.   [*LG* 33]

The question "What is the grass?" directs the eye of the Real
Me toward contact with a potential subject. His response will
have a pedagogical purpose. The Real Me will be one kind
of model for imitation, teaching the child by example how to
see "like men" the simplest particulars of the world. His work
is to transfer objects into a perspective of feeling and understanding. A projection of that aspect of mind which thinks in
analogies, and which consolidates rather than discriminates,
he will not speak of essences, nor categorize; the grass will be
drawn into his knowing on filaments of metaphor spun from
his intelligence and sensibility at the particular instant.

The motives for metaphor are as various as the contents of
the individual mind and will, and as the process of "knowing"
the object with the imagination proceeds in section 6, both
the sensibility and the ultimate concerns of the Real Me begin
to reveal themselves. The tenor of his first metaphor is pure
whim. The Real Me identifies the grass with his mood at the
moment, and the language is idiomatic, slangy, regional:

I guess it must be the flag of my disposition, out of hopeful
green stuff woven.   [*LG* 33]

The following "guesses" widen the metaphorical scope from
this incidental and fanciful identification to one responsive to
a universal human need for reassurance in the goodness of
things as they are. The tenor of the last metaphor in this section is a concept fundamental to the credo of the poem,
namely, that some vital and generous principle, in nature as
in the mind, wills, not the loss of things, but their transformation:

The smallest sprout shows there is really no death,
And if ever there was it led forward life, and does not wait
    at the end to arrest it,
And ceas'd the moment life appear'd.
All goes onward and outward, nothing collapses,
And to die is different from what any one supposed, and
    luckier. [*LG* 34–35]

The process of symbol-making conducted as if naively, in "guesses," by the newly invested hero at the beginning of the poem's action furnishes a paradigm of the larger structure of "Song of Myself." By just such processes of contact, mediation, and release will the Real Me by the end of his song have encompassed the entire world with his own identity, and transformed his temporality into something luckier.

As I observed earlier, the objects from reality which fill the long catalogues of sections 6–19 offer little resistance to the intrusive and absorptive imagination of the Real Me. During this phase he has selected for perusal "manifold objects" which his senses can trustworthily discover for him—the things which can be touched, heard, smelled, tasted and seen, and thus known, incorporated in form. During the next two phases of the action of "Song of Myself" the Real Me will have to encounter and befriend for poetry two subjects which are not so easily comprehended. These are libido—the primitive energies which lie just beneath consciousness and threaten the ego from within—and the processes of time and change which decree the ultimate loss of the self.

Sections 20–30

These sections of "Song of Myself" record the poet's discovery that the senses have a powerful dynamic of their own which opposes the imagination's will to form. The action begins in section 20 where the poet, having completed his survey

of "the grass that grows wherever the land and water is"
(*LG* 45), turns almost abruptly to the subject of himself:
"Who goes there? hankering, gross, mystical, nude." The answer is, "a man . . . solid and sound" whose own senses are
the only authorities he needs. Section 20 ends with what might
be regarded as an equivalent of the "battle boast" with which
the hero of epic ritually heartens himself for combat:

> My foothold is tenon'd and mortis'd in granite,
> I laugh at what you call dissolution,
> And I know the amplitude of time.   [*LG* 48]

The opponent of the Real Me here is not another hero,
however; it is the untrustworthiness of his own sensual nature.
The battle boast is succeeded by a group of long voluptuary
catalogues praising the body and fleshly appetites. In these
sections Whitman is asserting that the physical condition necessary to imaginative perception is, to borrow a term from
Norman O. Brown, "polymorphous perversity"—a filling of
the field of attention by all the senses at once. In the state of
consciousness Brown calls "polymorphous perversity" there
is an active interplay of the senses. Brown regards this state of
consciousness as the basis of metaphor, "the translation of all
our senses into one another." Brown distinguishes polymorphous perversity from "genital organization," the focusing of
attention on one part of the body alone; this he equates with
"spectatorship" and the deadening of creative energies.[27]

A similar conception seems to underlie the structure of this
phase of the action. In sections 21–25 the Real Me experiences
pleasure and pain with the whole of his body and with the
"female" capacities in himself as well as the "male":

> The pleasures of heaven are with me and the pains of hell are
> with me,

[27] Brown, *Love's Body* (New York: Random House, 1966), pp. 121,
249.

The first I graft and increase upon myself, the
latter I translate into a new tongue.
I am the poet of the woman the same as the man.   [*LG* 48]

[I] make short account of neuters and geldings, and favor
men and women fully equipt.   [*LG* 52]

Through me forbidden voices,
Voices of sexes and lusts, voices veil'd and I remove the veil,
Voices indecent by me clarified and transfigur'd.

. . . . .

If I worship one thing more than another it shall be the
spread of my own body, or any part of it,
Translucent mould of me it shall be you!
Shaded ledges and rests it shall be you!
Firm masculine colter it shall be you!
Whatever goes to the tilth of me it shall be you!

[*LG* 52–53]

This series culminates in section 25, where the Real Me explicitly refuses to grant sovereignty to any single mode of sense perception, recognizing that his creative power lies in their unifying interplay:

My knowledge my live parts, it keeping tally with the meaning of all things.   [*LG* 55]

At section 26, however, the disciplined integration of his faculties vanishes. He allows sovereignty to one of the senses, and is done in by its intensity. This occurs twice (in section 26 and in section 28); each time, the identity of the Real Me is crucially threatened. The crisis in 28, being sexual, presents the greater danger:

Is this then a touch? quivering me to a new identity,
Flames and ether making a rush for my veins,
Treacherous tip of me reaching and crowding to help them,

. . . . .

I am given up by traitors,

> I talk wildly, I have lost my wits, I and nobody else am the
>   greatest traitor,
> I went myself first to the headland, my own hands carried me
>   there.
>
> You villain touch! what are you doing? my breath is tight in
>   its throat,
> Unclench your floodgates, you are too much for me.
>
>   [*LG* 58]

Whitman reproduces a guilty sexual fantasy: the erogenous
zones become a herd of animals, the onrushing orgasm a terrifying predator. The guilt appears to derive from fears about
masturbation. But the metaphors carry several additional implications.

First, this section can be read as rendering a threat to what
Coleridge calls the "reconciling" influence of imagination, its
power to incorporate the reason in images of the sense, and
to organize the flux of the senses. For with the lines "I talk
wildly . . . my breath is tight in *its* throat" the Real Me reveals himself to feel separated from the body of the man. Myself, the "tallying" faculty mediating between sensation and
thought, has temporarily been replaced by a new identity
who is only erotic—just as in the preceding crisis, at section
26, he had been temporarily replaced by an identity who was
wholly a listener:

> The orchestra whirls me wider than Uranus flies.
>   . . . . .
> I am cut by bitter and angry hail, *I lose my breath,*
> Stupid amid honey'd morphine, *my windpipe throttled* in
>   fakes of death,
> At length let up again to feel the puzzle of puzzles,
> And that we call Being.   [*LG* 56; italics mine]

In these sections Whitman is structuring into "Song of Myself" the acknowledgment that libido is a realm ruled by a force more primitive than the civilizing will of the ego. The exaggerated claim for the primacy of sensation which he has been making throughout sections 20–25 is revealed as potentially destructive to poetry. These crises teach him that the imagination's strength is its power to *integrate* sensation with understanding. The Real Me must possess this intelligence before Whitman can make him a teacher of adolescents, as he does in the last phase of the poem's action.

Further, this pair of crises gains interest when juxtaposed. For each may be regarded as resulting from an overextension of one of the two modes of imagination, primary and secondary. In section 26 the imagination is primary, incorporative, as in certain preceding sections (see the catalogues of sections 8, 12, 13, and, particularly, 15). The incorporative identity remains intact until around line 596, when the Real Me begins listening to music. From line 601 on ("A tenor large and fresh as the creation fills me, / The orbic flex of his mouth is pouring and filling me full") the speaker is no longer Myself; he finds, indeed, that he does not recognize the self he has become ("It wrenches such ardors from me I did not know I posses'd them"—*LG* 56). As the effect of the music mounts he experiences again a climax resembling orgasm. This one, however, brings not a sense of self-completion and knowledge, as in section 5, but rather a sense of "the *puzzle* . . . that we call Being" (italics mine). When invoking his soul in section 5, Whitman specifically requested that it bring "[no] music or rhyme . . . not even the best, / Only the lull I like, the hum of your valvèd voice." Whitman consistently identifies the Real Me as his personal power of creativity, an identity relinquished when he becomes the recipient of another artist's forms, a mere member of an audience. The incorporative mode of imagination must avoid "absorbing . . . for this song" (*LG* 40) another man's words and music, lest these "throttle" the authentic voice of the Real Me.

The crisis of section 28 concerned the creation of an identity purely and powerfully phallic: "Treacherous tip of me reaching and crowding" (*LG* 57). The genital orientation which devastated the Real Me originated innocently enough in delighted exploration of masculinity as one resource of imagination; for a moment, the aroused phallus takes all his attention: "Firm masculine colter it shall be you! / Whatever goes to the tilth of me it shall be you!" (*LG* 53). The danger in this attentiveness, carried to its consummation, seems to be that the power to identify with the "female" in his human nature is half the creative power of the Real Me. Becoming all man, the speaker loses the universal Man in himself; hence the temporary separation of the Real Me from "the other I am."

I have suggested that the crisis to the identity of the Real Me dramatized in sections 26 and 28 results from the localization of sensual attentiveness in one of his sense organs, a state of consciousness which elicits pleasure but not poetry. The Real Me experiences this threat to identity as a loss of breath; inspiration ceases when the animal half of the man rises in anarchy against the powers of will and understanding which reconcile body with spirit. If Myself could not recover his voice, the poem would end. But in section 29 the Real Me demonstrates the process of reintegration which reconciles him to his animal nature. The term "reconciles" is precise here, for under the influence of libidinous sensation the Real Me has been tempted to distinguish "the best" in himself from the worst and to insist that his true identity lies somehow beyond rather than within his body. In section 29 his emotion of fear and self-rejection gives way to self-acceptance. Touch is perceived to be not some external stalking predator but a "blind" and "sharp-tooth'd" potential within the self. As horror turns to generosity, the unifying power of imagination returns, infusing sense data with the understanding, which organizes and interprets them. The recompense of surrender is insight into the creative process. The crisis mellows into metaphors that identify fertility in nature with just such surrender and recovery as the Real Me has mentally undergone in 28:

> Blind loving wrestling touch, sheath'd hooded sharp-tooth'd touch!
> Did it make you ache so, leaving me?

> Parting track'd by arriving, perpetual payment of perpetual loan,
> Rich showering rain, and recompense richer afterward.

> Sprouts take and accumulate, stand by the curb prolific and vital,
> Landscapes projected masculine, full-sized and golden.
>
> [LG 58]

Finally, I would like to observe, concerning these sections of "Song of Myself," that at the analogical level, where the poem may be said to be "about" imagination, this passage acknowledges the experience of a temporary loss of self-awareness as a necessary stage in the mental process that results in the creation of symbols. The primary act of imagination in its most significant form involves the destruction of an old order of knowledge—replacement of one workable generalization with another; and this feels to the Real Me like oncoming death or sleep. But it makes possible reintegration of thought and sensation at a new level of knowledge with new possibilities for formulation in poetry. This experience becomes Whitman's special subject in two poems of 1860, "As I Ebb'd with the Ocean of Life" and "So Long!", and I shall discuss it in detail with reference to them. It is also the concept implied in the tone and language of the next section-and-a-half of "Song of Myself," which begins with the statement, "All truths wait in all things." The ability to locate the general in the specific, the truth in the experienced thing, is token of the presence of primary imagination: a freshening of sight emerging from a temporary loss of discursive reason under the powerful grip of sensation. Body is not more than soul and soul is not more than body. Temporarily relinquishing its primacy, the soul, or power of intellection, allows for the refreshment of sensation, the state in which, according to Coleridge, ideas become "immediate":

> Logic and sermons never convince,
> The damp of the night drives deeper into my soul.   [LG 58]

At the exclusive poles of either sensation or ideation in Whitman, selfhood is lost; but as sensation submits to discursive understanding, or reason burgeons within a state of ecstatic sensation, the Real Me arises again, articulate in the mind of the living man. Hence, the conclusion of this phase in the action comes with the "drop of me" into the aroused senses, infusing them with generalized meaning:

> All truths wait in all things,
> They neither hasten their own delivery nor resist it,
> They do not need the obstetric forceps of the surgeon,
> The insignificant is as big to me as any,
> (What is less or more than a touch?)
>
> A minute and a drop of me settle my brain,
> I believe the soggy clods shall become lovers and lamps,
> And a compend of compends is the meat of a man or woman,
> And a summit and flower there is the feeling they have for
>   each other,

And they are to branch boundlessly out of that lesson until
  it becomes omnific,
And until one and all shall delight us, and we them.

I believe a leaf of grass is no less than the journey-work of
  the stars. [LG 58–59]

Sections 31–38

In the calm, reflective mood that settles over him after the
crises dramatized in the preceding sections, the Real Me turns
his thought to the animals—"They are so placid and self-con-
tained." They do not resist their own nature as he has done,
as all men do, so they make good models of imitation for the
animal half of a man. Gazing with love upon other creatures
(sections 31–32), the Real Me suddenly perceives "tokens of
myself," a perception which becomes an insight into the duration and continuity of his own character:

I wonder where they get those tokens,
Did I pass that way huge times ago and negligently drop
  them?

Myself moving forward then and now and forever,
Gathering and showing more always and with velocity.
                                                    [LG 60]

This intuition shapes the third phase of action in "Song of
Myself."

Space and Time! now I see it is true, what I guess'd at,
What I guess'd when I loaf'd on the grass,
What I guess'd while I lay alone in my bed,
And again as I walk'd the beach under the paling stars of the
  morning. [LG 61]

The above lines recall the sites of two of the earlier ventures in self-exploration which the Real Me has undertaken, and indicate the arena of the third: the concepts of space and time as they bear on the questions of individual suffering and mortality. Whitman's purpose is to locate the mental perspective from which these terrifying human facts may be regarded without despair.

Before I go on to discuss this phase, however, it will be useful to remark briefly on the organization of the whole poem to this point. As every commentator notices, the structure of Whitman's argument is rhythmic rather than logical, reflecting the ebb and flow of psychic energies. The "flowing," or intrusive, movement of the mind in "Song of Myself" corresponds to what Coleridge identifies as the unifying mode of secondary imagination; the opposite movement carries the mind inward to ideation, musing, self-absorption—back to the state of perception which Coleridge considers to be primary. Further, during its withdrawal into the primary phase the imagination accumulates confidence in the truth of its discoveries; each retreat is followed by a bold return to the intrusive, form-finding secondary mode. These two movements are characterized by significant alterations in style. The primary mode is meditative, reflective, and generalizing in content:

> So they show their relations to me and I accept them,
> They bring me tokens of myself, they evince them plainly
>   in their possession.   [LG 60]

The secondary mode results either in short parables (sections 6 and 11, for example) or in the catalogue technique, the lengthy particularizing of observed details which support and amplify the poet's generalizations. The structure is not rigid or symmetrical in character, and the shift from the primary to the secondary mode does not necessarily correspond to section divisions: some sections alternate line by line. But it may be observed that the longer catalogues appear at intervals, in response to the important self-discoveries I have been identifying here, and always succeed brief generalizing "primary" intervals. Hence in the first phase of the action of "Song of Myself" the important primary intervals may be identified as 6–7 and 16–19; the secondary interval as 8–15. The primary intervals in phase two are 20, 23, 25, 27, 29–30. During the primary phases the poet "announces" his subject, or, alternatively, he summarizes it and draws conclusions. Out of numerous examples I cite a few favorites:

> This is the meal equally set, this the meat for natural hunger,
> It is for the wicked just the same as the righteous, I make
>   appointments with all. [LG 46]

> I know I am solid and sound,
> To me the converging objects of the universe perpetually
>   flow,
> All are written to me, and I must get what the writing means.
>   [LG 47]

> I find I incorporate gneiss, coal, long-threaded moss, fruits,
>   grains, esculent roots,
> And am stucco'd with quadrupeds and birds all over,
> And have distanced what is behind me for good reasons,
> But call anything back again when I desire it. [LG 59]

In the secondary phase the poet demonstrates the applicability of his perceptions; he is afoot with his vision—"reducing multiety to unity" (Coleridge, *Biographia Literaria*, XV). The effect of his discoveries, large or small, is cumulative. As he comes to understand the extent of his power to incorporate diverse objects, the horizon of his mental cosmos expands. At section 20, he had abandoned the mode of joyful attentiveness to the appearances of external objects (sections 6–19) to probe the question "What is a man anyhow? / What am I? what are you?" (*LG* 47). At section 33, having explored the autocosmic boundaries of his own body (sections 20–30), the Real Me turns to the theme of the macrospheric boundlessness of space and time.

"Now I see it is true what I guess'd at," Whitman begins; "What I guess'd when I loaf'd on the grass, . . . while I lay alone in my bed" (*LG* 61). The lines direct our attention back to section 6, which I have described as a paradigm of the symbol-making that occurs in the poem, a demonstration of the way experience becomes image and is saved from nature by art. We are intended to observe, I think, that the sprouts transplanted from life have taken and accumulated; they now stand before us, man-sized, in the poem. What the poet guessed at, alone, under the influence of the soul, has now become part of our minds; his consciousness comes alive again within our own as we turn his leaves.

The capacity of intellect which has allowed him to do this is his power to perceive typicality. If he loves the animals because they are "self-contain'd," he loves himself better because he is not:

> I but use you a minute, then I resign you, stallion,
> Why do I need your paces when I myself out-gallop them?
> Even as I stand or sit passing faster than you.   [*LG* 61]

Accepting his animal half has permitted him now to look beyond it, and to observe that the long process of natural evolution has worked tirelessly to produce that power of intelligence which can detect sameness in difference—the ground of metaphor. Whitman now dramatically enlarges the human image to gigantic proportions:

My ties and ballasts leave me, my elbows rest in sea-gaps,
I skirt sierras, my palms cover continents,
I am afoot with my vision.   [*LG* 61]

Rearing vast and expectant over the hemisphere that supports him, the Real Me is an impressive figure. But he is not yet complete as the socially oriented epic hero of "Song of Myself."

Up to this point the Real Me has been occupied with discovering the sheerly personal satisfactions to be derived from the act of form-finding that is his work as a personification of imagination. The truth he now has guessed is that his transformations convert *experience* into verbal *meanings*, making them communicable to other men. The relevance of the leaves of grass is not private but transcontinental; wherever man is, has been or will be, his words mean. The Real Me is about to absorb for the poem the concept which E. D. Hirsch, in his valuable study *Validity in Interpretation*, defines as the principle of "sharability" in linguistic structures.

Verbal meaning can never be limited to a unique, concrete content. It can, of course, refer to unique entities, but only by means that transcend unique entities, and this transcendence always has the character of a typification. This is so even when a verbal meaning has reference to something that is obviously unique, like "the death of Buonaparte." "Death," "the," and "of" all retain their type character even though their combination might effect a particular new type. The same is true of "Buonaparte," for a name is a type, and the particular name "Buonaparte" could not relinquish its type character without thereby ceasing to be a name, in which case it would be incomprehensible and unsharable. No doubt this particular name in a particular use would not have a meaning identical to "Buonaparte" in another usage. But that would simply mean that they are different types as well as, on another level, instances of the same type. However, they could never be merely concrete instances. The determinacy and shar-ability of verbal meaning resides in its being a type.[28]

This point about sharability is made by Whitman in an "act of finding" as the secondary imagination takes over for the poem the insight that the Real Me is the verbal identity of actual things, and that his life is the life of language rather than of time-bound flesh. Two kinds of literary form are generated. One is catalogue (section 33), the longest and most ambitious in "Song of Myself," as for 154 lines the Real Me sweeps through time and space discovering his presence everywhere, in the very *names* of things. The second form is anecdote. The Real Me recounts two tales, verbal structures in which types of human significance are preserved in culture, outliving their occasions (sections 34–36). Like other kinds of folk art these anecdotes have a quality of formal naiveté, but they are firmly literary in design, nonetheless; and notes to the poem indicate that Whitman freely sacrificed fact to euphony or verisimilitude.[29]

The crisis in this phase of the action develops out of the power of imaginative forms to evoke "the willing suspension of disbelief for the moment which constitutes poetic faith."

[28] Hirsch, *Validity in Interpretation* (New Haven: Yale University Press, 1968), p. 28.

[29] In retelling the massacre by the Mexican enemy of Captain Fannin and his men at Goliad in March 1836, Whitman alters the number slain from three hundred seventy-one to "four hundred and twelve," dropping two syllables and redistributing the stresses. In 1836 Whitman would have been seventeen and had not visited Texas; one assumes he read about the massacre in the papers. The editors also note that while Whitman first heard the tale of the sea-fight from his maternal grandfather, who had served under John Paul Jones, his own account closely parallels the account made by Jones in a letter to Benjamin Franklin, printed in *Old South Leaflets* (Boston, n.d.), VII, 36–39. See *Leaves of Grass, Comprehensive Reader's Edition*, n. 875 and n. 899, pp. 68–69.

In the sections that render the crisis (37–38), Whitman seems to be working with the assumptions about the artist which form the basis of Thomas Mann's story "Tonio Kröger." Tonio, the alienated Romantic, describes the creative process this way:

If you care too much about what you have to say, if your heart is too much in it, you can be pretty sure of making a mess. You get pathetic, you wax sentimental; something dull and doddering, without roots or outlines, with no sense of humour—something tiresome and banal grows under your hand, and you get nothing out of it but apathy in your audience and disappointment and misery in yourself . . . feeling, warm, heart-felt feeling, is always banal and futile. . . . The artist must be unhuman, extra-human; he must stand in a queer aloof relationship to our humanity; only so is he in a position, I ought to say only so would he be tempted, to represent it, to portray it to good effect. The very gift of style, of form and expression, is nothing else than this cool and fastidious attitude towards humanity.[30]

What Mann describes, Whitman dramatizes in sections 33–38, where the mastery of the Real Me over his subject lasts only so long as he maintains the distinction between feeling and its literary formulations. In section 33 he has firm control of the distinction; if not "cool and fastidious," he is at least rather aloof: "Agonies are one of my changes of garments . . . I lean on my cane and observe" (*LG* 67). Loss of control occurs gradually, as empathic analysis turns to pity, then fear. This development and its resolution are the subject of sections 36–38, and can be characterized in brief excerpts from those sections. The Real Me has been describing a violent battle at sea. His account concludes with

[30] Mann, *Stories of Three Decades*, trans. H. T. Lowe-Porter (New York: Knopf, 1936), p. 103.

> The hiss of the surgeon's knife, the gnawing teeth of his saw,
> Wheeze, cluck, swash of falling blood, short wild scream,
>   and long, dull, tapering groan,
> These so, these irretrievable.

Suddenly, as if overwhelmed by the power of his own narrative, he exclaims:

> You laggards there on guard! look to your arms!
> In at the conquer'd doors they crowd! I am possess'd!
> *Embody* all presences outlaw'd or suffering,
>
> . . . . .
>
> Enough! Enough! Enough!
> Somehow I have been stunn'd. Stand back!
> Give me a little time beyond my cuff'd head, slumbers,
>   dreams, gaping,
> I discover myself on the verge of a usual mistake.
>
> [*LG* 70–72; italics mine]

The disequilibrium and consequent panic Whitman describes is analogous to what psychologists call "play disruption." Play, according to Erik Erikson, is the practice of ego mastery in an "intermediate reality," one that lies between fantasy and actuality. The person at play constructs model situations offering problems that have to be solved according to strict but arbitrary rules. For play to continue until the problems are solved and the ego's mastery affirmed, the player must preserve a degree of emotional uninvolvement; as Erikson puts it, he must feel free of any fear or hope of serious consequences.[31] When an emotion aroused by play becomes so intense that it defeats "playfulness," the ego is threatened and the player turns defensively against the situation he had a moment before pleasurably controlled. Applying Erikson's definition to the situation rendered in sections 36–38 of "Song

---

[31] Erikson, *Childhood and Society*, p. 212.

of Myself," we may observe that the "mistake" the Real Me
finds himself about to make is failure to maintain the perspective of play. His subject matter in this third phase of action
has been mortality and human suffering. As a poet, his accommodation to the subject must be formal; he must manage and
transform these actualities until they yield meaning, and give
to the human beholder the pleasure of intelligibility. The feeling of ego mastery lasts for the Real Me only while he maintains the elegist's distance from grief, employing to that end
literary techniques available in the genres of ballad and folk
tale, patterning response in accordance with the kinds of resolution these genres afford.

The Real Me, further, is a man at play in public. His work
is the construction of culturally viable models of resolution in
which complexes of experience grow coherent, wishes are
reconciled with actuality. His purpose is to give pleasure of
the particular sort identified by Coleridge as the pleasure of
"immediacy" to "the shadowy abstraction of living and actual
truth" (*Biographia Literaria*, XII). He performs his play as
a model, for the sake of other men, winning them to a wise
love of things as they are. Whitman dramatizes the resolution
of this identity crisis as a reawakening of intelligence:

> That I could forget the mockers and insults!
> That I could forget the trickling tears and the blows of the
> bludgeons and hammers!
> That I could look with separate look on my own crucifixion
> and bloody crowning.
>
> I remember now,
> I resume the overstaid fraction,
> The grave of rock multiples what has been confided to it, or
> to any graves,
> Corpses rise, gashes heal, fastenings roll from me.
> I troop forth replenish'd with supreme power, one of an
> average unending procession.   [*LG* 72]

The Real Me recovers as the power to generalize returns, restoring the notions of typicality, recurrence, averages, and the relations of parts to wholes. Whitman draws his metaphors from the world of business: to overstay one's fraction in a market is to stay with a transaction beyond the point at which the greatest profit might have been taken. The poet's capital is the immediacy of sense experience; his proper work is to manage and transform that experience in the context of an artificial reality, one made of words. To be successful he must "forget" something of the actual suffering his art seeks to reveal. By such means does his experience become meaning, sharable verbal structures detached from the unique occasions which are the source, as well as the test, of their value.

Sections 39–47

By the end of section 38 the education of the Real Me is complete. "Now the performer launches his nerve," he will say as the last phase begins, "he has pass'd his prelude on the reeds within" (*LG* 76). Before discussing the sequence which proves the epic significance of Whitman's hero, however, it will be useful to summarize the principles which I have been describing in Coleridge's terminology as the ideology shaping the hero's sense of his role.

First, the Real Me is an effort to characterize in significant *actions* the human abstract Emerson describes in "The American Scholar":

There is One Man—present to all particular men only partially, or through one faculty; and you must take the whole society to find the whole man. Man is not a farmer, or a professor, or an engineer, but he is all. Man is priest, and scholar, and statesman, and producer, and soldier. In the *divided* or social state these functions are parcelled out to individuals, each of whom aims to do his stint of the joint work, whilst each other performs his. The fable implies that the individual, to possess himself, must sometimes return from his own labor to embrace all the other laborers. But, unfortunately, this original unit, this fountain of power, has been so distributed to multitudes, has been so minutely subdivided and peddled out, that it is spilled into drops, and cannot be gathered.[32]

"—Cannot be gathered," Emerson means, except in the mind, by means of recognizing the aspect of universality in one's own particular experience. In that moment of recognition the One Man looks through the mortal eyes of Individual Man and knows himself to span the centuries. His origin is the first human consciousness developed in organic matter. And, as a dynamic of physical and psychological growth patterns arrayed before the nervous system acquired human form, determined by the natural laws which govern organic matter and decree death, the One Man recurs in every new body born.

The Real Me, however, is not the whole of the One Man, but Man Voicing. He is the flesh made word, composed of the verbal meanings salvaged by intellect from sensibility at every stage of human growth from birth to death. He is also the aspect of mind conscious of similitude; hence he can rise free from feelings of alienation and fear of the unknown. Finally, the Real Me is a circumscribed hero. The only mode of action available to him is mental: he is pure self-consciousness. Yet that becomes the rationale according to which Whitman offers him, in the last phase of action in "Song of Myself," as hero of the epic of democracy. So far in this discussion I have been describing the Real Me as the personification of a theory of imagination for which the ultimate source is

---

[32] Emerson, "The American Scholar," *Works*, I, 82–83.

Coleridge, and emphasizing the degree to which "Song of Myself," like Wordsworth's *Prelude,* applies that theory in a chronicle tracing the growth of the poet's mind. Whitman's motives in composing "Song of Myself," however, were revolutionary and nationalistic. As he wrote in the 1855 preface to *Leaves of Grass,* and in countless self-explanatory letters throughout his life, he hoped in his poetry to establish for his countrymen a new model of Man. His effort to do so in "Song of Myself" is traditional to the extent that its informing epistemology is Romantic and its formal structure resembles epic. But Whitman's conception of his hero departed radically from any previous model available in fiction or poetry. The Real Me has no stable community; he lives in no particular place; and no parent, wife, friend, or child appears in influential connection with him. He has no politics, no religion and, strictly speaking, no profession—he makes his poems while loafing, and, unlike Whitman, never writes them down. Nonetheless he is offered in "Song of Myself" as what Stevens has called "the central man," a character ideal or model for imitation. Whitman offers him thus on the basis of the insight that in an ideal democratic society, where the common man is made the authorizer of both social and private action, and where hierarchies are unstable, the ideal ethical character would belong to the man capable of maintaining a viable morality by mediating the pressure of instinct from within and the demands of social existence from without.[33] The Real Me is the verbal expression of that mediation, translating into conscious meaning both the pressures and their legitimate deflec-

[33] My reading of Whitman here was influenced significantly by Philip Rieff's interesting commentary on "psychological man" in *The Triumph of the Therapeutic* (New York: Harper and Row, 1966), especially pp. 31–32.

tions. We have watched him in the first three phases of the poem develop just this imaginative ethical consciousness. In the last phase Whitman releases him into a social context, making him the articulate embodiment of Democratic Man.

The final phase of action in "Song of Myself" has two movements. In the first, sections 39–43, the Real Me conceives a new mode of relation to his subject. During the first three phases the creative energies of the Real Me were primary: like the lady at the window in his parable (section 11), the Real Me was all eye; his mode of contact was visual and "absorptive." In this fourth phase his identity has become, through absorption, complete, as he acknowledges in section 44:

> All forces have been steadily employ'd to complete and delight me,
> Now on this spot I stand with my robust soul.   [LG 81]

From section 38 on, the creative energies of the Real Me are "secondary": he is all breath and voice, the principle of coherence and integrity which fills interstices and draws diversity into perspectives of unity. He no longer absorbs; he invests:

> I seize the descending man and raise him with resistless will,
> O despairer, here is my neck,
> By God, you shall not go down! hang your whole weight upon me.
>
> I dilate you with tremendous breath, I buoy you up.
>   [LG 74]
>
> Magnifying and applying come I,
>   .   .   .   .   .
> Accepting the rough deific sketches to fill out better in myself.   [LG 75]

Be at peace bloody flukes of doubters and sullen mopers,
I take my place among you as much as among any,
The past is the push of you, me, all, precisely the same.

[LG 79]

This altered form of the Real Me reflects his intuition about what his role is to be in the new culture of his country. His intuition enters the poem at section 39, in the image of the "friendly and flowing savage," native of the New World, who moves among his fellow men bestowing forms of selfhood:

Wherever he goes men and women accept and desire him,
They desire he should like them, touch them, speak to them, stay with them.

Behavior lawless as snow-flakes, words simple as grass, uncomb'd head, laughter, and naivetè,
Slow-stepping feet, common features, common modes and emanations,
They descend in new forms from the tips of his fingers,
They are wafted with the odor of his body or breath, they fly out of the glance of his eyes.   [LG 73]

The reference to words "simple as grass," together with the emphasis on breath and eye, identify this figure as a self-projection of the Real Me, one which incorporates his discovery that his role in culture is to serve in the shaping of a national identity. What he will offer to the "eleves" he has invited to cluster around him is an embodiment in language of "manhood, balanced, florid and full" (section 44). This social function, he goes on to observe in sections 41–43, is the democratic equivalent of the role filled historically by hierarchies of priests; and it is a social role created in response to a continuing human need for images of completion, man's "old inexplicable query" (section 42) concerning his origins and his end.

The second movement of this phase begins at section 45. The Real Me here begins to take possession of the bodies of other men, imposing his form on theirs and uncovering theirs in his. He ushers his human subjects into himself with a gesture of delight, admitting them through the porches of every sense:

> My lovers suffocate me,
> Crowding my lips, thick in the pores of my skin,
> Jostling me through streets and public halls, coming naked to
>   me at night,
> Crying by day *Ahoy!* from the rocks of the river, swinging
>   and chirping over my head,
> Calling my name from the flower-beds, vines, tangled under-
>   brush,
> Lighting on every moment of my life,
> Bussing my body with soft balsamic busses,
> Noiselessly passing handfulls out of their hearts and giving
>   them to be mine.   [*LG* 81–82]

He performs this act of mutual identification on the basis of his Emersonian perception that mankind is actually One Man, an "elastic" compendium of life at every stage from the "span of youth" to "Old age superbly rising." The Real Me in this section perceives humanity as an immense collage, a vast macrocosm which, superimposed on nature, gives the universe a human form, one made in the image of the Real Me.

> Wider and wider they spread, expanding, always expanding,
> Outward and outward and forever outward.
>
> My sun has his sun and around him obediently wheels,
> He joins with his partners a group of superior circuit,
> And greater sets follow, making specks of the greatest inside
>   them.   [*LG* 82]

This symbolic representation of the One Man as a dynamic integration of human culture in any instant of time bears sig-

nificant resemblance to Stevens' "Primitive Like an Orb," a
human figure projected on the horizon of culture, who embodies spiritual ideals and stands as model for the makers of
images—"the lover, the believer, and the poet." These image-
makers, Stevens writes, have in common that

> Their words are chosen out of their desire,
> The joy of language, when it is themselves.
> With these they celebrate the central poem,
> The fulfillment of fulfillments, in opulent,
> Last terms, the largest, bulging still with more,
>
> Until the used-to earth and sky, and the tree
> And cloud, the used-to tree and used-to cloud,
> Lose the old uses that they made of them,
> And they: these men, and earth, and sky, inform
> Each other by sharp informations, sharp,
> Free knowledges, secreted until then,
> Breaches of that which held them fast. It is
> As if the central poem became the world.   [CP 441]

Stevens is claiming here that the verbal symbol conveys not
only the outlines of the object to which it refers, but the spirit
of its speaker as well; possessing the poem we momentarily
internalize realities which were before wholly external, and
we participate in the sensibility whose perceptions gave rise
to the symbol. A significant enough maker of words, Stevens
goes on to say, can encompass an entire culture within his
generous and accessible sensibility, and become the articulated
human figure upon which elevated sight converges:

> It is a giant, always, that is evolved,
> To be in scale.
>
>   · · · · ·
>
> And still angelic and still plenteous,
> Imposes power by the power of his form.

Here, then, is an abstraction given head,
A giant on the horizon, given arms,
A massive body and long legs, stretched out,
A definition with an illustration, not
Too exactly labelled, a large among the smalls
Of it, a close, parental magnitude,
At the centre on the horizon, concentrum, grave
And prodigious person, patron of origins.   [CP 442–443]

I have quoted at length from Stevens' expository poem because it articulates the concept of the cultural function of poetry which Whitman approaches by indirection in these last sections of "Song of Myself." The Real Me becomes in the final movement of the poem precisely Stevens' giant: "a close parental magnitude . . . impos[ing] power by the power of his form." The Real Me takes his eleves and lovers by hand or waist and draws them with him along a path of consciousness which articulates in them a knowledge of their own selfhood. This is the action toward which the whole poem has been tending, and it occupies relatively few lines; it is dramatized in section 46 and reiterated in the catalogue of 47.

The vehicle of Whitman's thought in section 46 is the metaphor of journeying which in 1856 became the central symbol of two important poems, "Song of the Open Road" and "Crossing Brooklyn Ferry."

I tramp a perpetual journey, (come listen all!)
My signs are a rain-proof coat, good shoes, and a staff cut
    from the woods,
No friend of mine takes his ease in my chair,
I have no chair, no church, no philosophy,
I lead no man to a dinner-table, library, exchange,
But each man and each woman of you I lead upon a knoll,

My left hand hooking you round the waist,
My right hand pointing to landscapes of continents and the
    public road.   [*LG* 83]

Several details in this representation receive significant development in the course of the next two sections of "Song of
Myself." First, the Real Me does not make himself a leader of
other men. He and his companions are conceived as equals.
The significant difference between them is his attained maturity: the Real Me is the abstracted Being in any Becoming,
flesh made word. His contact is made, as usual, by way of
touch. But this is the touch of secondary imagination, the
power of form-finding; it invests the mind with articulate intelligence. In the company of the Real Me the mind moves to
an elevated perspective—here a knoll—from which small particulars may be perceived in terms of their relation to each
other in a larger whole. The point of view arrived at under
the influence of the Real Me, however, does not focus on
particulars in a landscape. The Real Me offers himself as a
model of right self-consciousness, not as a model of action—
poet, scholar, businessman, hospitable host. His sole function
is to raise other men "flush with myself," completing in the
mind an articulated self-image answerable to the demands of
the moment.

Not I, not anyone else can travel that road for you,
You must travel it for yourself.

It is not far, it is within reach,
Perhaps you have been on it since you were born and did not
    know.   [*LG* 83]

Since the Real Me is a man made of words he needs no
battleground on which to perform his epic task. Every mind
is his *patria:*

I follow you whoever you are from the present hour,
My words itch at your ears till you understand them.

[*LG* 85]

He does his work in any time or place, literally brought to
life in the thoughts of men and women who carry him along
in pockets, sea-chests, bedrolls or memory—as Whitman is re-
ported to have carried Emerson's essays along while working
at odd jobs in carpentry, to read at lunch. At section 47, before bequeathing himself to silence, Whitman takes a last ten-
der look at the common life—One Man in his and her many
social functions—and everywhere hears his own words moving
in rhythms like a heartbeat in the consciousness of the New
World:

The young mechanic is closest to me, he knows me well,
The woodman that takes his axe and jug with him shall take
    me with him all day,
The farm-boy ploughing in the field feels good at the sound
    of my voice,
In vessels that sail my words sail, I go with fishermen and
    seamen and love them.

The soldier camp'd or upon the march is mine,
On the night ere the pending battle many seek me, and I do
    not fail them,
On that solemn night (it may be their last) those that know
    me seek me.

My face rubs to the hunter's face when he lies down alone in
    his blanket,
The driver thinking of me does not mind the jolt of his
    wagon,
The young mother and the old mother comprehend me,
The girl and the wife rest the needle a moment and forget
    where they are,
They and all would resume what I have told them.

[*LG* 85–86]

And finally, the Real Me forms no community with his companions, envisions no establishment which includes the initiated and excludes the unregenerate. His relation to other men is, by his definition as secondary imagination, temporary. It involves a momentary completion of intelligence in a mind abstracted from practical considerations; but the state of knowingness has no duration, it is merely a phase in an ongoing process of intellection. This is a point so important to the poem's meaning that Whitman did not rely on indirection for its statement in section 46:

> This day before dawn I ascended a hill and look'd at the crowded heaven,
> And I said to my spirit *When we become the enfolders of those orbs, and the pleasure and knowledge of everything in them, shall we be fill'd and satisfied then?*
> And my spirit said *No, we but level that lift to pass and continue beyond.*   [LG 83–84]

The Real Me believes that laws inhere in the order of things but become living *truths* only when made immediate within the context of experienced particulars. The mind formulates or realizes truth in a context of time, so that the eternal knowingness projected by the speaker is rejected by his "spirit" or intellectual authority, as a false idea. The mind, like the cosmos, expands and expands from a point locatable in childhood, in the earliest discriminations of similitude made by the individual intelligence. ("How could I answer the child?" Whitman has asked; "I did not know any more than he.") This process goes on as long as breath survives; and though interrupted by the living man's periodic relaxation into sleep or habit, the Real Me, or active imagination, is resumed in every mind motivated to draw abstract law into the sphere of living reality. The large pleasure this action yields, Whitman claims, is the human absolute which makes irrelevant the notion of a superhuman absolute; it is the fact in experience for which the name God is the vehicle in metaphor:

> And I say to mankind, Be not curious about God,
> For I who am curious about each am not curious about God,
> (No array of terms can say how much I am at peace about God and about death.)

> I hear and behold God in every object, yet understand God not in the least,
> Nor do I understand who there can be more wonderful than myself.

> Why should I wish to see God better than this day?
> I see something of God each hour of the twenty-four, and each moment then,
> In the faces of men and women I see God, and in my own face in the glass,
> I find letters from God dropt in the street, and every one is sign'd by God's name,
> And I leave them where they are, for I know that wheresoe'er I go,
> Others will punctually come for ever and ever.   [*LG* 86–87]

Whitman completes the poem's mythic plot at section 46. We have seen how, in the opening lines of this section, Whitman has established that the relation of the Real Me to other men is as a temporary companion on the path to a point overlooking a wide prospect—"landscapes of continents and the public road." Now the Real Me turns, and for the first time in the poem addresses another human being:

> Shoulder your duds dear son, and I will mine, and let us hasten forth.   [*LG* 83]

This sentence introduces the mild denouement of the action;

within twelve lines the Real Me will "open the gate for your egress hence" and send the young man out of sight. The action will be complete, save for the hero's farewell. The twelve lines addressed to the "dear son" express Whitman's insight that Democratic Man is necessarily a solitary resident of the sphere of possibility. This is the burden of the hero's only words to his charge:

> If you tire, give me both burdens, and rest the chuff of your
>   hand on my hip,
> And in due time you shall repay the same service to me,
> For after we start we never lie by again.
>
> . . . . .
>
> You are also asking me questions and I hear you,
> I answer that I cannot answer, you must find out for yourself.
>
> . . . . .
>
>   as soon as you sleep and renew yourself in sweet
> clothes, I kiss you with a good-bye kiss and open the gate
> for your egress hence.
>
> Long enough have you dream'd contemptible dreams,
> Now I wash the gum from your eyes,
> You must habit yourself to the dazzle of the light and of
>   every moment of your life.
>
> Long have you timidly waded holding a plank by the shore,
> Now I will you to be a bold swimmer,
> To jump off in the midst of the sea, rise again, nod to me,
>   shout, and laughingly dash with your hair.   [LG 83–84]

The young man must educate himself through contact with the secondary imagination in its completed forms—the nourishing "bread of faithful speech" the Real Me offers here and that Stevens offers the soldier at the conclusion of *Notes toward a Supreme Fiction* (CP 408). But the last lesson the spiritual father of his nation offers his progeny is the wise disengagement from established forms: the way of imagination. Through disinheritance from the culture of the past the spiritual son achieves his own manhood: the power to master any medium and to generate new forms within it, keeping the Real Me in existence for posterity.

Closure: It Must Change
Sections 48–52

With the gesture of dismissal performed lovingly in section 46 Whitman initiates the conclusion of his poem, in the course of which the Real Me begins to fade, lose energy and articulateness, and at last to slip away into sleep or death. This movement fills sections 48–52. The Real Me first summarizes the ideology of his song (48) in generalizations that become, in Coleridge's sense, less and less "immediate":

> I have said that the soul is not more than the body,
> And I have said that the body is not more than the soul,
> And nothing, not God, is greater to one than one's self is.
>
> [*LG* 86]

Darkness falls at section 49, and in 50 the Real Me settles as if to rest amid a group of sentence fragments suggesting oncoming sleep:

> There is that in me—I do not know what it is—but I know it is in me.

> Wrench'd and sweaty—calm and cool then my body becomes,
> I sleep—I sleep long.

> I do not know it—it is without name—it is a word unsaid,
> It is not in any dictionary, utterance, symbol.   [*LG* 88]

At 52, the Real Me departs, returning his breath to air and his body to water and earth.

I depart as air, I shake my white locks at the runaway sun,
I effuse my flesh in eddies, and drift it in lacy jags.

I bequeath myself to the dirt to grow from the grass I love,
If you want me again look for me under your boot-soles.

[*LG* 89]

This is an effective conclusion. Its effect derives partially
from the decorum which prescribes that a biographical fiction
end with the death of the subject under study. It derives too
from the poem's ideology. To the extent that "Song of Myself" is an allegory of imagination, Whitman is here acknowledging that the self projected in the poem is an abstraction
from life, vulnerable to the claims of life. The intellectual
energies of Walt Whitman the poet are called away from his
persona the Real Me by nature, vested in the spotted hawk
who "swoops by and accuses me . . . complains of my gab
and my loitering" (*LG* 89). The poet "dies" back into reality
as the poem ends.

But more than this, he disinherits himself from a completed
form. As the real man returns to life, the Real Me returns to
immanence, becoming potential rather than realized in the
mind. As invested secondary imagination, he has taken the primary abstraction on which the poem rests ("the hand of God
is the promise of my own, . . . And limitless are leaves stiff
or drooping in the fields") and carried it to its fulfillment in
aesthetic form. Now—to recall Coleridge's definition—he dissolves, diffuses, and dissipates himself, awaiting re-creation in
the active intelligence of another shaper of leaves: whether
Whitman on another day, or anyone, "you."

"*The Sleepers*"

"Song of Myself" and "The Sleepers" were published the

same year, in the first edition of *Leaves of Grass* (1855), where "The Sleepers" was the fourth of twelve poems. In 1860, when Whitman began redesigning *Leaves of Grass* with an idea of its total structure in mind, "The Sleepers" was moved toward the back of a book that now contained over 150 poems. The new order seems to have been based on a model from nature. It is dawn when the poet begins his fabulous voyage in *Leaves of Grass*, 1860:

> [Having] heard at dawn the unrivall'd one, the hermit thrush
>   from the swamp-cedars,
> Solitary, singing in the West, I strike up for a New World.
> [*LG* 16]

The last poems in that volume are meditations on night, sleep, death, silence. This rearrangement of the poems, while structurally effective, conceals the fact that "Song of Myself" and "The Sleepers" were composed before 1855, in the period of Whitman's greatest interest in the persona of the Real Me, and disguises the thematic similarities of the two poems. In the fiction of the Real Me, "Song of Myself" may be regarded as the poem of daylight consciousness which places the heroic identity in his social context. The hero of "Song of Myself" is a solitary, as we have seen, but the poem is epic in design and feeling; it seeks to convey the mythic dimensions of American character and to envision a destiny. "The Sleepers" is a poem of nighttime consciousness, which reveals the poetic identity in its purely private context. The dreaming narrator, "lost to myself" (*LG* 425), wanders in the chaos of the psyche's underground, confronting his anxieties one by one. These confrontations progressively unman him, until he is rescued by that aspect of imagination which can transform the energy of fantasy into the energy of coherent symbolism.

In "The Sleepers," the Real Me transforms personal anxiety into art.

To summarize the poem's narrative: the action takes place in the dark, until section 7, when light, perhaps dawn, slightly rouses the dreamer and redirects the stream of his sleeping thought. The images have the quality of being spotlighted, picked briefly out of the darkness. Throughout, restless sleep is skillfully suggested, as is the vulnerability of the dreams to the slightest stimulus. Thus the long erotic passage in section 1 fades away on a reference to what may be the dreamer's own heart throbbing in passionate response to the dark lover:

> Be careful darkness! already what was it touch'd me?
> I thought my lover had gone, else darkness and he are one,
> I hear the heart-beat, I follow, I fade away.   [LG 427]

The structure of the poem may be seen as a linear movement downward to darkness through ever more troubling and highly detailed dream experience until the middle of section 5, where helplessness and grief in the face of death become, in sections 5–6, nostalgia and sorrow in the face of departure. At section 7, a new motion enters; the descent into the dark begun in section 2 becomes "sailing" and "flowing" in the "dim light" through the rest of the poem, until it is "rich-running day" (LG 433) and the dreamer is about to awaken.

The dream images with which I am first concerned occur with the descent of the "lost to myself" dreamer. Passing among the sleeping bodies that crowd the opening lines, he chooses to *stand* "by the worst-suffering and the most restless" (LG 425). He drifts briefly through several identities before becoming, in a long passage, she who "adorn'd herself and folded her hair expectantly"—and who, in the mode of sleeping eroticism, attempts but fails to reach a climax of contact and fulfillment:

> My hands are spread forth, I pass them in all directions,
> I would sound up the shadowy shore to which you are jour-
>   neying. [*LG* 427]

This slippage through other identities ends when he becomes
a shroud and lies in a coffin, at the farthest remove from joy
and hope, but where it is dark and "blank . . . for reasons"
(*LG* 427). There, apparently, he stays, to dream most intensely: now not a participant by identification, but a helpless
spectator. And what he dreams, three times, seems to be the
death of the self to which he is lost, though that self goes
disguised or is generalized into beautiful and well-beloved
comrades. The physical characteristics of the ideal "Myself"
celebrated in the "Song" seem clearly recognizable, however,
in the first of these dreams, in the "beautiful gigantic swim-
mer swimming naked" and about to be killed "in the prime of
his middle age" (*LG* 428). Like the harassers of the "Me
myself" in "Song of Myself" the waves torment the swim-
mer. But the waves are more violent than the forces in the
"Song"; the giant drowns.

The second dream is identified ambiguously as "a past-read-
ing, another," perhaps to indicate that Whitman as journalist
actually witnessed a drowning and a shipwreck, or their after-
math. However, the point of likeness between this dream and
the one preceding lies in the profound grief aroused in the
dreamer as an uncontrollable sea takes its victims. Whitman futilely tries to share their suffering, since he cannot prevent it:

> I cannot aid with my wringing fingers,
> I can but rush to the surf and let it drench me and freeze
>   upon me. [*LG* 429]

In the third dream the emotion of helpless grief is displaced
onto another figure, General Washington. Displacement opens

the dreamer's way out of his grave. Liberated from total identification with his emotion, the dreamer can begin to manage,
control, and interpret the details of the image. The mediation
of feeling by understanding that enters at section 5 tokens the
presence of creative imagination; and its reconciling power
takes over the poem now, beginning at section 6:

> Now what my mother told me one day as we sat at dinner
>   together,
> Of when she was a nearly grown girl living home with her
>   parents on the old homestead.
>
> A red squaw came one breakfast-time to the old homestead,
> On her back she carried a bundle of rushes for rush-bottom-
>   ing chairs,
> Her hair, straight, shiny, coarse, black, profuse, half-envelop'd
>   her face,
> Her step was free and elastic, and her voice sounded exqui-
>   sitely as she spoke.
>
> My mother look'd in delight and amazement at the stranger,
> She look'd at the freshness of her tall-borne face and full and
>   pliant limbs,
> The more she look'd upon her she lov'd her.
>   . . . . .
> O my mother was loth to have her go away,
> All the week she thought of her, she watch'd for her many
>   a month,
> She remember'd her many a winter and many a summer,
> But the red squaw never came nor was heard of there again.
>   [LG 429–430]

This dream ends, like the others, in the permanent loss of a
beloved object. But one detail has transformed the pattern of
anguish and frustration represented before. This dream-ex-

perience has been rendered into a narrative, with its beginning
and end resolved into an aesthetic whole; and it has entered
the dreamer's consciousness *as* an aesthetic whole, or symbol.
In the symbol the loss endured "many a winter and many a
summer" (*LG* 430), having been given order and sense in
the mother's mind, operates as a value. It creates a mode of
sympathetic communication between mother and son many
years later, and, further, has a reality in his mind correspondent to the memory in hers.

The dream about the squaw is not interpreted in the poem:
Whitman's method is indirect. But it is the poem's turning
point, and the interpretation I have given is indicated in the
turn the poem takes. The dreamer's helpless passivity abates.
Energy returns with the dawn. The opening lines of section 7
convey the dreamer's intuition of a change. Liberation and
joy become his new destination.

> Elements merge in the night, ships make tacks in the dreams.
> [*LG* 430]

The dreamer is about to extricate himself by a series of ma-
neuvers resembling the tacks a sailor, going into the wind,
makes to reach a point already perceived but still some distance away. The dreamer's voyage is through a sea of images.
All the images which previously caused him grief and pain
are summoned again. Again he enters the sleepers' dreams,
and this time he finds dreams of fulfillment, with every wish,
even the most impossible, satisfied. He anchors his mind with
this statement:

> The antipodes, and every one between this and them in the
> dark,
> I swear they are averaged now—one is no better than the
> other,
> The night and sleep have liken'd them and restored them.

I swear they are all beautiful,
Every one that sleeps is beautiful, every thing in the dim
light is beautiful.   [LG 431]

The meaning of these lines is elusive. But in the action of
the poem, the dream of the dreamer's return from the grave,
they represent the intercession of the creative aspect of the
mind, a *fiat* of the soul, as the dreamer is aware. The "contact
of something unseen" referred to in the first line of this section turns out to have been the soul, in its aspect as the imagination. "Every thing in the dim light is beautiful" now because the soul has come, and

The soul is always beautiful.
      . . . . .
It cames from its embower'd garden and looks pleasantly on
itself and encloses the world.   [LG 432]

It penetrates with knowledge and peace the sleeper's confu-
sion and the inexplicability of his dreams, and without rob-
bing them of their particularity it draws them into a splendid
coherence:

The universe is duly in order, every thing is in its place,
What has arrived is in its place and what waits shall be in its
place.
      . . . . .
The diverse shall be no less diverse, but they shall flow and
unite—they unite now.   [LG 432]

The remainder of the poem affirms the soul's operation in the
dreamer's mind, causing the world to flow with images of re-
union. The relation between each pair of sleepers of section 8
is a fulfilled version of the relation between the powerless
dreamer and his lost comrades:

Learn'd and unlearn'd are hand in hand, and male and female
are hand in hand,

.The bare arm of the girl crosses the bare breast of her lover,
they press close without lust, his lips press her neck,
The father holds his grown or ungrown son in his arms with
measureless love, and the son holds the father in his arms
with measureless love,
The white hair of the mother shines on the white wrist of
the daughter.   [*LG* 432]

The aging Whitman often spoke of the soul as of a trust-
worthy servant, subject to his bidding.[34] But in "The Sleepers"
soul is still one of the names of creative imagination. Its function is to consolidate the man's creative power; when the soul
enters the mind, Walt Whitman becomes the Real Me, the self
capable of knowledge, sympathy, and control—even in the
ominous regions of nightmare.

"As I Ebb'd with the Ocean of Life"

In *The Dyer's Hand*, W. H. Auden sketches the biography
of a hypothetical poet. He brings the young poet to the day
his internal Censor says "truthfully and for the first time: 'All
the words are right, and all are yours.' " This is not the happy
ending it appears, though.

For a moment later comes the thought: "Will it ever happen
again?" Whatever his future life as a wage-earner, a citizen, a
family man may be, to the end of his days his life as a poet will
be without anticipation. He will never be able to say, "Tomorrow I will write a poem and, thanks to my training and experience, I already know I shall do a good job." In the eyes of others
a man is a poet if he has written one good poem. In his own he is
only a poet at the moment when he is making his last revision to

---

[34] "Come forward O my soul, and let the rest retire, / Listen, lose
not, it is toward thee they tend" (*LG* 403).

a new poem. The moment before he was still only a potential poet; the moment after, he is a man who has ceased to write poetry, perhaps forever.[35]

This episode in Auden's fictive biography of a poet prefaces discussion of the poet's Muse, by Auden called, after Coleridge, the primary imagination. A major premise of that discussion is that the faculty which makes for poetry is *passive*. The young poet cannot know whether he will write another poem, we infer, because the mind cannot will to find the poetic object, or as Auden calls it, the "sacred being"—"the sacred being cannot be anticipated: it must be encountered." Further, upon encountering it, "the imagination has no option but to respond."[36]

So far I have dealt with the equivalents in Whitman's poetry of this capacity for being "found" by one's poetic objects as the operation of the *soul*, because so far only the prophetic or "exemplary" poems have been involved—the poems wherein Whitman mythologizes the imagination's ability to bestow grace on ordinary life. That is the kind of poetry Whitman wanted to write, as he announced in all his prefaces and in many of the poems too; and "Song of Myself" is the greatest achievement of this aspiration. The poem I want to deal with next presents, from one angle of vision, an exact reversal of sections 1–5 of "Song of Myself."

"As I Ebb'd with the Ocean of Life" expresses Whitman's anxieties about whether he is really the poet he says he is. The poem records the discovery that the Real Me as personified in "Song of Myself" is a fiction. As at the opening of "Song of Myself," the poet describes himself as awaiting inspiration. "Held by this electric self out of the pride of which I utter

[35] Auden, *The Dyer's Hand* (New York: Random House, 1962), p. 41.

[36] *Ibid.*, p. 55.

poems," the poet is again loafing and musing, thinking "the old thought of likenesses, . . . seeking types" (*LG* 253–254). In "Song of Myself," however, the season was "a transparent summer morning" (*LG* 33); now it is "late in the autumn day" (*LG* 253), and the spirit that comes to invest the poet with creativity is harsh and fearful: "[I] was seized by the spirit that trails in the lines underfoot, / The rim, the sediment" (*LG* 253–254). The poet has been chosen by this spirit, as Auden would say, and has no option but

> to follow those slender windows,
> Scum, scales from shining rocks, leaves of salt-lettuce left by the tide,
> Miles walking.   [*LG* 254]

Throughout the rest of the poem the voice of "I" comes from the tidewrack washing the shore, speaking its meanings. This is the key to the point of view from which we see the images: the Real Me, and later, "you" the reader, is positioned above "I" looking down on him. For the Real Me enters this poem as an unsympathetic critic of the narrator:

> Aware now that amid all that blab whose echoes recoil upon me I have not once had the least idea who or what I am,
> But that before all my arrogant poems the real Me stands yet untouch'd, untold, altogether unreach'd,
> Withdrawn far, mocking me with mock-congratulatory signs and bows,
> With peals of distant ironical laughter at every word I have written,
> Pointing in silence to these songs, and then to the sand beneath.   [*LG* 254]

In section 3 the poet, full of anguish, submits his will to the idea that all he has written is dead; and he begins to seek help from two archetypal sources of regeneration: the ocean, personified as "the fierce old mother," and the island Paumanok, "my father."

Since the poet's relation to these is analogous to his relation with the soul in "Song of Myself," it is important to identify their meanings before proceeding to discuss their roles in the last half of the poem. Ocean is represented here as a voice from the sea, "hoarse and angry" (*LG 255*), that cries, moans, and sobs the "dirge of Nature" (*LG 256*). She is represented variously as the voice of the drowned corpses she contains, or as their mourner; her expression is of the lowest order of imagination, a simple emotional cry of loss, endlessly repeated —dirge as opposed to elegy. At the beginning of the poem she is at a distance, an ominous element in the background, but at 2 she emerges as a force with which the poet must reckon:

> As I list to the dirge, the voices of men and women wreck'd,
>
> · · · · ·
>
> The ocean so mysterious rolls toward me closer and closer.
>
> [*LG 254*]

Elsewhere in his poetry Whitman vividly imagines his own death by drowning. Here ocean's hostility is a secondary theme, overshadowed because the poet has bequeathed his voice to the sea, or more specifically, to the rim of the sea where the tidewrack collects. At section 3, then, he "closes" with ocean[37] as a token of his recognition that, having failed to touch the Real Me, his songs have actually been as elementary and limited as ocean's cry—

[37] The line here is "You oceans both, I close with you" (*LG 255*). The other ocean was specifically identified in the first published version of the poem as "You tangible land! Nature!", though Whitman's meaning is not substantially clarified either by the identification of its exclusion. "Both" probably remained in the line for the sake of its rhythm.

> We murmur alike reproachfully rolling sands and drift,
> knowing not why,

—for which the dead leaves are an adequate symbol:

> These little shreds indeed standing for you and me and all.
> [*LG* 255]

As for the island: Paumanok's shore is for Whitman a sacred place. He withdraws there for meditation on the "vast
similitudes" of things, the "clef of the universes."[38] In "Out
of the Cradle," Paumanok's "gray beach" is the sacred territory on which he learns his poetic destiny; hence he "starts"
from Paumanok for a new world in the poem that significantly precedes "Song of Myself" in the final arrangement of
Leaves of Grass. In "As I Ebb'd with the Ocean of Life," the
surge of creative energy that carried the "outsetting bard"
forward is now at ebb, a history condensed into a single line:
"I too have bubbled up, floated the measureless float, and been
wash'd on your shores" (*LG* 255). He returns to the island
as to "shores I know, seeking types," and the island does not
fail to furnish them:

> Chaff, straw, splinters of wood, and the sea-gluten.
>   . . . . .
> These you presented to me you fish-shaped island.
> [*LG* 254]

With the details of this summary in mind, it can be seen
that the personifications of ocean as mother and island as father refer back to the sources of poetry as represented elsewhere in Whitman. The gesture of closing with ocean has
two meanings. The first has already been mentioned: the poet
identifies with the sea's voice as the crier of loss—the only

[38] "On the Beach at Night Alone" (*LG* 260).

authentic mode of speech possible in this ebb of confidence. But he also returns to her as to a mother from whom new life can be won:

> Endlessly cry for your castaways, but fear not, deny not me,
> Rustle not up so hoarse and angry against my feet as I touch
>   you or gather from you.

> I mean tenderly by you and all,
> I gather for myself and for this phantom looking down
>   where we lead, and following me and mine.   [*LG 255*]

Richard Chase has identified the multiple ambiguities of Whitman's image of the fierce but maternal sea. "The idea of loss is . . . converted from water to mother and then generalized, by way of the symbolic connection of mother and sea as well as by the poet's memories of his early love and fear of the sea, to include that inconceivable but sublime sense of loss incident to the emergence of life itself from the all-encompassing waters. In this manner Whitman grasps at the most poignant center of experience, and it is characteristic of him that where other poets would be likely to derive the meaning of life and the origin of imagination from God . . . Whitman . . . derives them from death."[39] "As I Ebb'd with the Ocean of Life," like "Out of the Cradle," speaks of the birth of poetry out of the knowledge of death. The poet does not emerge from the sea in this poem—in fact he visualizes himself as a corpse rolling in the tide—but he submits to her for reasons hinted at toward the end: that life and poetry are "out of fathomless workings fermented and thrown" (*LG 256*).

The poet's dealings with the hoarse and hostile mother are only half the poem's ending. His hopes for a new birth reside in the father, in whose personification we can again recognize

[39] Chase, *Walt Whitman Reconsidered* (New York: William Sloane, 1955), pp. 122–123.

the visage of Whitman's "soul" or principle of intelligence. The poet approaches him with a gesture that is the inversion of the soul's act in "Song of Myself":

> I throw myself upon your breast my father,
> I cling to you so that you cannot unloose me,
> I hold you so firm till you answer me something.
>
> Kiss me my father,
> Touch me with your lips as I touch those I love,
> Breathe to me while I hold you close the secret of the mur-
>   muring I envy.   [LG 255]

"The Sleepers" ended with a promise to night and darkness: "I know not how I came to you and I know not where I go with you, but . . . [I will] duly return to you" (LG 433). "As I Ebb'd with the Ocean of Life" is the courageous fulfillment of it. The lines surrounding "I close with you," "I take what is underfoot," are Whitman's version of

> Those masterful images because complete
> Grew in pure mind, but out of what began?
> A mound of refuse or the sweepings of a street.
>
>   . . . . .
>   Now that my ladder's gone,
> I must lie down where all the ladders start,
> In the foul rag-and-bone shop of the heart.
>   [Yeats, "The Circus Animals' Desertion"]

Despite its elegaic tone, "As I Ebb'd with the Ocean of Life" affirms that the poet knows the origins of authentic art. Having submitted to the vision of the "spirit that trails in the lines underfoot," the poet begins to regain a position of power with reference to the "unreach'd" Real Me. He gathers the discarded images from the sea "for myself and for this phantom looking down where we lead and following me and mine" (LG 255). The Real Me represented in the discarded leaves is a fiction; as he appeared in "Song of Myself" he has been outgrown. He and the poet disown each other in this poem, and the poet's grief at losing him fills every line. But "As I Ebb'd" shows the poet at another stage of life from that recorded in "Song of Myself," and the poem is an expression of desire to find the authentic voice for that changed state. The Real Me, represented here as the authentic poetic consciousness in the role of censor—the consciousness who prevents Whitman from writing badly—must condemn poetry that fails to "tally" him. But on the other hand, the Real Me is only a phantom in the poet's mind until he achieves life in accurate speech.

"So Long!"

"So Long!" is Whitman's epitaph for the Real Me. It might have been titled "The Last Song of Myself," for it speaks symbolically of the exhaustion of one subject for poetry, and intimates that the next tiding of the creative cycle will beach the poet on different shores from the ones he has known.

Choosing the moment "While my pleasure is still at the full," the poet—"dying"[40]—gathers energy to celebrate himself for the last time: "Hasten throat and sound your last, / Salute me" (*LG* 505). The hectic song which follows proves to him that he is still the powerful channel of the great theme:

[40] Gay Wilson Allen believes that Whitman really thought in 1860 that he might write no more: "The failure of the second or third editions to win recognition had so discouraged the poet that in *So Far and So Far* (No. 20 in the Leaves of Grass section), which was never again published in his lifetime, he confessed his wavering ambition: 'whether I continue beyond this book to maturity . . . [depends upon] you, contemporary America.'" *Walt Whitman Handbook* (Chicago: Packard, 1946), p. 146.

> Curious envelop'd messages delivering,
> Sparkles hot, seed ethereal down in the dirt dropping,
> Myself unknowing, my commission obeying, to question it
> never daring. [*LG* 505]

But also that he can carry it no further; everything has been said:

> What is there more, that I lag and pause and crouch extended
> with unshut mouth?
> Is there a single final farewell?
>
> My songs cease, I abandon them. [*LG* 505]

The poem ends with speculations about the translation of his consciousness into new forms:

> I feel like one who has done work for the day to retire
> awhile,
> I receive now again of my many translations, from my ava-
> taras ascending, while others doubtless await me,
> An unknown sphere more real than I dream'd, more direct,
> darts awakening rays about me, *So long!* [*LG* 506]

The point being made in "So Long!" is that the real man has literally been translated into the poems.

> Camerado, this is no book,
> Who touches this touches a man. [*LG* 505]

Echoing the enigmatic promises at the end of "Song of Myself," Whitman asserts that within his songs he is permanently accessible, "really undying," in the only way he has ever aspired to be:

> The best of me then when no longer visible, for toward that
> I have been incessantly preparing. [*LG* 505]

The center of "So Long!" then, reads like a conscious recantation of the dread in "As I Ebb'd with the Ocean of Life" that the Real Me was never reached. And the last lines of the poem—"I am as one disembodied, triumphant, dead"—affirms that in the cycle outward from Paumanok and back the Real Me has been "fully made, fully apparent, fully found." These words were written not by Whitman but by Wallace Stevens;[41] and it was also he who said that the "supreme fiction," or myth that gives this solid order to a world of being, "must change" (CP 389). In a sense, this is intimated in "So Long!" in the announced abandonment of an accomplished mode. But Whitman did not rise to the new order of imagination "more real than I dream'd, more direct" (LG 506) that the poem projects. The poem also projects, however, a departure "from *materials*" (italics mine), and lists at its beginning a slate of abstractly democratic topics for the poetry of the future, which would be nationalistic in theme, optimistic in tone. A note written just before his death acknowledges the attenuated quality of his poetic inspiration: " 'I do not suppose that I shall ever again have the afflatus I had in writing the first *Leaves of Grass* [an experiment] out of the abysms of the Soul.' "[42] "So Long!" however, was written in anticipation of the failure of primary imagination to breathe again "the secret of the murmuring I envy." It is an epitaph designed to memorialize the passing of the Real Me, the inspired consciousness described once in "Song of Myself" as

Walt Whitman, a kosmos.   [LG 52]

[41] "Credences of Summer" (CP 376).
[42] Quoted in the editors' introduction, *Leaves of Grass, Comprehensive Reader's Edition*, p. xxvii.

Chapter 2

The Hero Afoot with His Vision

The land and sea, the animals, fishes and birds, the sky of heaven and the orbs, the forests, mountains and rivers, are not small themes . . . but folks expect of the poet to indicate more than the beauty and dignity which always attach to dumb real objects . . . they expect him to indicate the path between reality and their souls.

—Preface to *Leaves of Grass,* 1855

Toward the end of "Song of Myself" Whitman said of his poems, "It is you talking just as much as myself, I act as the tongue of you, / Tied in your mouth, in mine it begins to be loosen'd" (*LG* 85). A major intention of "Song of Myself" (and, by implication, the whole 1855 volume) was to create an exemplary American hero, on the democratic assumption that all men were really poets if only they knew it. For poets, according to Whitman's definition, were simply men who could define the relation between external objects and the imagination, "the path between reality and their souls."

The heroic potential of the act of imagination is the theme of Whitman's preface to *Leaves of Grass,* 1855. There Whitman, like Emerson before him and Stevens after, discusses the act of "right knowing" as the most significant human act, and the poet as the man most likely to perform it: most capable, therefore, of becoming the hero of a modern democratic culture. The imagination of such a "bard" (as opposed to that of a mere "singer")[1] would have to be central rather than eccentric: "of all mankind the great poet is the equable man" (*LG* 712); but it would also have to possess individuality and power of insight greater than the common: "High up out of reach he stands turning a concentrated light" (*LG* 713); "He glows a moment on the extremest verge" (*LG* 716). His poetry is meditative and affirmative, what Stevens called "the poem of the mind in the act of finding what will suffice" (*CP* 239). Of what Stevens calls "the act of finding," itself, Whitman has few definitions in the preface or even in the poems published with it. But many of the most interesting poems of the editions that followed in 1856 ("Song of the Open Road," "Crossing Brooklyn Ferry," "Spontaneous Me") and in 1860 ("Out of the Cradle Endlessly Rocking," "Scented Herbage of My Breast") were written to demonstrate the heroic aspect of imagination and the role it plays in culture. In the following pages I shall examine in chronological order poems which show the poet enacting his social role: liberating common folk into their identities as poets of their own experience.

"Song of the Open Road"

"Song of the Open Road," published in 1856, celebrates the incorporative power of primary imagination. It is organized, like "Song of Myself" (and almost all of the poems in the canon of the Real Me), by the metaphor of journeying, but its difference from that poem is indicated in the title. The poet here is unconcerned with his own identity; he is completely self-possessed:

[1] See "Song of the Answerer": "The singers do not beget, only the Poet begets" (*LG* 169).

> Afoot and light-hearted I take to the open road,
> Healthy, free, the world before me,
> The long brown path before me leading wherever I choose.
>
> [*LG* 149]

Whitman's subject is the "lesson of reception" that the road has to teach. The poem is dominated by two ideas about the transaction between reality and imagination: that the mind must be receptive—that is, not closed by preconception—and that reality contains implicit "existences" waiting to enter into relation with the receptive mind.

The first of these ideas is expressed in terms familiar from other Whitman poems, and appears chiefly in the exhortation to abandon books, libraries, all the paraphernalia of institutional education; come into the open air where "a great *personal* deed has room" (italics mine); to enter reality "and look around" (*LG* 149). It is linked to a larger theme of passing on, leaving things behind, giving things away. Whitman means that a man must be unprepared or "ignorant," in Wallace Stevens' special sense,[2] if he would step into reality as poet. He must be unconcerned with material possessions (section 11) or with the formulas and dogmas of "bat-eyed priests": those are the corpses of the past (section 10) and no fit companions. He must enter reality only with his own identity at the full of power (section 5). For on the open road one is permitted neither to prefer nor to deny (section 18); one must simply be open-eyed and in motion.

The kind of intellectual innocence and openness Whitman proposes in "Song of the Open Road" is the clearing of the

---

[2] See "The Sense of the Sleight-of-Hand Man": "It may be that the ignorant man, alone, / Has any chance to wed his life with life" (*CP* 222); also *Notes toward a Supreme Fiction*, "It Must Be Abstract": "You must become an ignorant man again, / And see the world again with an ignorant eye" (*CP* 380).

mind to induce the state of primary imagination, when the soul is most receptive to reality. The whole theme of the poem is celebration of such receptivity, suggesting that when the aggressive and intrusive modes of the ego are relinquished, a great resource becomes available to the mind:

> From this hour I ordain myself loos'd of limits and imaginary lines,
> Going where I list, my own master total and absolute,
> Listening to others, considering well what they say,
> Pausing, searching, receiving, contemplating,
> Gently, but with undeniable will, divesting myself of the holds that would hold me.
>
> . . . . .
>
> I am larger, better than I thought,
> I did not know I held so much goodness.   [*LG* 151]

In this poem Whitman places the highest value on change (motion) and on the pressures of "unseen existences" moving into the opened mind. During the transaction between "I" and reality, meaning is created. Whitman says it more simply: "Objects . . . call from diffusion my meanings and give them shape!" (*LG* 150). Further, the experience of contact with things is the only real wisdom, or knowledge of truth. It "cannot be passed from one having it to another not having it" because it is *of* the self and hence "is its own proof." It consists of "the certainty of reality." "Something there is in the float of the sight of things that provokes it out of the soul," and a man is made real:

> Here is realization,
> Here is a man tallied—he realizes here what he has in him.
>   [*LG* 152]

Finally, all such certainties are possessed only at the instant of the encounter and are outgrown the next: "However wel-

come the hospitality . . . we are permitted to receive it but
a little while" (*LG* 154), Whitman says. The whole point of
the journey is summarized in the line, "What beckonings of
love you receive you shall only answer with passionate kisses
of parting" (*LG* 155). Yet while nothing is taken nothing is
lost; there is "no possession but you may possess it, enjoying
all without labor or purchase, abstracting the feast yet not abstracting one particle of it" (*LG* 156).

"*Crossing Brooklyn Ferry*"

"Song of the Open Road" attempts to describe what happens in the encounter between reality and the soul, or imagination. "Crossing Brooklyn Ferry," another poem of the 1856
Leaves of Grass, extends these insights to the world realized
within the poem. "Crossing Brooklyn Ferry" begins more or
less where "Song of the Open Road" ends, with the certainty
that a man is sustained "at all hours of the day" by acts of
primary imagination: sustained both by ideas which enter the
mind as metaphors—"similitudes of the past and those of the
future"—and by experience flooding the senses as "glories
strung like beads on my smallest sights and hearings" (*LG*
160). This is the soul's wisdom in "Song of the Open Road,"
proof that "the earth is sufficient." But in "Crossing Brooklyn
Ferry" Whitman meditates on the larger question of the *shar-
ability* of meaning: the realization of a world within a poem
which makes it susceptible to realization within the mind of a
reader. "Crossing Brooklyn Ferry" has a large purpose: to
articulate a theory of imagination in which self and reality are
viewed as merging in a form that transcends mortality and
links mind to mind in a timeless communal bond.

Whitman's symbol for reality in this poem is the East River
separating Brooklyn from Manhattan, which, being subject to

tides, partakes of all the advantages for metaphor of both river and sea. In its dazzle, its motion, and its equivalence in the poem to sheer Being, it bears comparison with Wallace Stevens' symbol of the Connecticut River,[3] for the poet offers it as the ultimate of reality yielding to sense, so that as Stevens said, "It is not to be seen beneath the appearances that tell of it" (*CP* 533). That is, Whitman's river does not exist in the poem apart from the perceiver who has entered into relation with it.

> Flood-tide below me! I see you face to face!
> Clouds of the west—sun there half an hour high—I see you also face to face.
>
> Crowds of men and women attired in the usual costumes, how curious you are to me!
> On the ferry-boats the hundreds and hundreds that cross, returning home, are more curious to me than you suppose,
> And you that shall cross from shore to shore years hence are more to me, and more in my meditations, than you might suppose.   [*LG* 159–160]

Eventually, the elaborated symbol of the river and onlooking soul is made to serve as answer to the central problem of the poem, posed as a question in section 5: "What is it then between us?" (*LG* 162). One aspect of the symbol posits the river as the enduring context of being that furnishes the basis of similarity between individual lives; since the modes of perception are alike in all men, all are capable of being sustained, as the poet is sustained, by entering into relation with the world of objects. "Time nor place [nor] distance avails not" to diminish this certainty, because no matter when you live, Whitman asserts, "the bright flow" can "refresh" you (*LG* 160). To this belief is linked the idea that identity comes via

---

[3] Cf. "The River of Rivers in Connecticut" (*CP* 533).

the body, that a man realizes himself in and is perpetually re-
created by imaginative experience: "That I was I knew was
of my body, and what I should be I knew I should be of my
body" (*LG* 162). If men have similar experience they are
bound to have, at some level, similar identities. But both of
these clues to the relation between "I" and "you" in the poem
have reference to the actual world of crossers of Brooklyn
Ferry, and the poem is, after all, addressed to a reader. What
connects the "bright flow" of the real and the created worlds?

Whitman avoids answering that question in "Crossing
Brooklyn Ferry" because the poem is supposed to work without explaining itself: "What I promised without mentioning
it, have you not accepted?" he asks near the end. But underlying his hints is an idea of the poet explored in yet another
poem of 1856 and later titled "Song of the Answerer." Men
come to the Answerer with messages they are unable to interpret and with questions about each other they are unable
to resolve. The Answerer encounters the questioner face to
face, and things become clear: "in him [they] perceive themselves as amid light" (*LG* 166). He answers them with signs;
his gift is the ability to translate encounters with reality into
symbols, and thus enable other men to encounter reality. He
can do this because "Every existence has its idiom, every thing
has an idiom and tongue, / He resolves all tongues into his
own and bestows it upon men, and any man translates, and
any man translates himself also" (*LG* 168). This pattern—if
not the description—of "answering" is repeated in "Crossing
Brooklyn Ferry." Particularly important is the metaphor of
being "face to face." At the beginning of the poem the poet
is face to face with the river, and at the end the subtle thing
that "ties me to the woman or man that looks in my face" is
made equivalent to the nameless thing "which fuses me into
you now, and pours my meaning into you" (*LG* 164). But

of course the reader is not face to face with Whitman;[4] if the
enterprise has been successful he is face to face with the poem.
"I" is the poem. As in "So Long!" the poet's triumph is the
creation of an identity eternally capable of reception by the
mind—though that identity now belongs to the world of objects, is a possible "Thou," and not an "I." This is acknowledged in another poem of 1860, "Full of Life Now," from the
Calamus group:

> When you read these I that was visible am become invisible,
> Now it is you, compact, visible, realizing my poems, seek-
>   ing me,
>
> . . . . .
>
> Be it as if I were with you.   [*LG* 136]

In "Crossing Brooklyn Ferry," however, the emphasis is not
so much on this translated identity as on the world of appearances which may, if their idioms have been rightly given
tongue, "now or henceforth indicate what [they] are" (*LG*
165). The poem is a heterocosm, a world in which the meanings have already been realized by a receptive mind. The real
world and the translated world are thus both implicated in the
concluding lines of praise:

> You have waited, you always wait, you dumb, beautiful
>   ministers,
> We receive you with free sense at last, and are insatiate hence-
>   forward,
> Not you any more shall be able to foil us, or withhold your-
>   selves from us,

---

[4] Though given Whitman's interest in the possibility of the existence of a transcendent spiritual world, it is necessary to allow that
he might have intended these lines to be taken literally. For interpretation of the nature of Whitman's belief in immortality, see James
E. Miller, Jr., *A Critical Guide to Leaves of Grass* (Chicago: University of Chicago Press), pp. 126–129.

We use you, and do not cast you aside—we plant you per-
   manently within us,
We fathom you not—we love you—there is perfection in you
   also,
You furnish your parts toward eternity,
Great or small, you furnish your parts toward the soul.

[LG 165]

But perhaps the translated world is praised most. "Crossing
Brooklyn Ferry" implies that a poem creates a world never
so real as when it has become sharable. This is only hinted at,
in such details as the claim that appearances will *henceforth*
indicate what they are; but it is powerfully implied in the
spectre of the Unreal Me admitted at section 6, the schizo-
phrenic identity, always aware of himself as two, who fails
to yield up his silence even when called by his "nighest name."
"I . . . / Saw many I loved in the street or ferry-boat," Whitman says of him, "yet never told them a word" (*LG* 163).
In "Crossing Brooklyn Ferry" he tells them.

One more feature of the path between reality and the soul
remains to be considered before we are through with these
two poems, and that is the importance of movement. The voyage metaphor is the fundamental organizing device in both
"Song of the Open Road" and "Crossing Brooklyn Ferry,"
and it has significant roles even in poems it does not control,
such as "Out of the Cradle Endlessly Rocking" and "When
Lilacs Last in the Dooryard Bloom'd." But it belongs to the
theoretical as well as to the structural aspects of Whitman's
poetry. The Romantic concept of reality taken over by Whitman through Emerson is based on a view of nature as process.
The relation between the mind and a symbolic structure—the
world perceived in correspondences or a work of art embody-
ing that world—is conceived as dynamic. Such a symbolic
structure, as one critic has remarked, "has no fixed or static

meaning but changes with the observer in a relationship between the two which is both dialectical . . . and organic."[5]
Section 6 of "Song of Myself"—"A child said, *What is the
grass?* fetching it to me"—perfectly illustrates this principle.
The child knows as well as Whitman, for the grass is not
known at all except in the mind's transactions, and the changes
in the mind confronting it make continual changes in its
meaning. All the metaphors for the grass are equally true. At
the same time, the grass itself is changing with the light and
air, and by sprouting, burgeoning, and dying off, is ever re-
newed for the mind. Reality washes like waves over consciousness, and what it leaves are regarded as gifts possessed
for an instant. While the event of bestowal passes, the soul
never loses what was given. The gift of reality becomes part
of itself, the soul is altered by it. At the same time, the soul is
in motion confronting reality; its gifts are also of itself. This
reciprocal encounter, creative for both self and reality, is expressed in two lines of "Song of Myself":

> This is the far-off depth and height reflecting *my own face*,
> This is the thoughtful merge of myself, and the outlet again.
> [*LG* 46; italics mine]

The quality of divinity attributed to "I" by the end of
"Song of Myself" is the product, then, of the complete identification of reality with self as depicted in "Crossing Brooklyn Ferry." The poet is the self or life of reality, its capacity
for relation with human consciousness. In "Song of the Open
Road," where "I" and reality are *not* one but are viewed in a
relation of reciprocity, Whitman describes their capacity for

[5] Morse Peckham, "Toward a Theory of Romanticism," *PMLA*,
LXVI, 229–253. Peckham's reference is specifically to the work of
art; but my extension of it to the act of perception is in line with his
discussion of the Romantic idea of the mind as "radically creative,"
and with his discussion of the creative mind.

relation as an "efflux." The efflux of reality "pervades the open air, waiting at all times"; when it flows into us "we are rightly charged" (*LG* 153). The efflux of the mind is primary imagination yearning toward, or questioning, reality, desiring to come face to face with reality. Seeking a fuller meaning, Whitman calls this capacity in both reality and the soul "The fluid and attaching character," and finds one correspondence for it in the natural growth of the grass in response to the sun:

> The fluid and attaching character is the freshness and sweetness of man and woman,
> (The herbs of the morning sprout no fresher and sweeter every day out of the roots of themselves, than it sprouts fresh and sweet continually out of itself.)   [*LG* 154]

Whitman is no more analytical than this about "the path between reality and the soul": "Something there is in the float of the sight of things" (*LG* 152). That is all the Real Me knows about it, for his whole identity is the capacity of the living mind for intense responsiveness. The "fluid and attaching character" of the soul is a *donnée* of being; when "it flows into us, we are rightly charged" (*LG* 153), and poetry is a natural product:

> Spontaneous me, Nature,
>
> . . . . .
>
> Beautiful dripping fragments, the negligent list of one after another as I happen to call them to me or think of them,
>
> . . . . .
>
> And this bunch pluck'd at random from myself,
> It has done its work—I toss it carelessly to fall where it may.
> [*LG* 103–105]

When the soul fails to come "from within through embower'd gates . . . provoking questions" (*LG* 153) the Real Me no longer exists. But that dark fact is irrelevant to Whitman's myth of the hero's power during the period 1855–1856, when he possesses it at the full, with "the merge of Myself and the outlet again" in a voyage through time.

"Out of the Cradle Endlessly Rocking"

The poems of 1855–1856 discussed above represent the poet as a liberator of consciousness. By example and by exhortation the poet teaches his fellow men how to translate life into communication, to transform experiences into words which survive their occasions, and convey, through generation after generation, the meanings of things. In "Out of the Cradle Endlessly Rocking," which appeared in the third edition of *Leaves of Grass*, Whitman records the liberation of his own "tongue's use" (*LG* 251). The fiction of the Real Me as developed in "Song of Myself" ideologically rejects as sources of liberation either reading books or paying attention to teachers; hence in Whitman's mythic autobiography no human mediator intervenes to free the actual man to become the Real Me, the man made of words. Rather, the momentous discovery of *meaning*, "the path between reality and the soul," is described as a wholly natural event that took place in childhood sometime near puberty.

The beautiful opening passage of "Out of the Cradle," with its movement "Out . . . Out . . . Over . . . Down . . . Up . . . From . . ." (*LG* 246–247), may be compared to Whitman's earlier poem about childhood, "There Was a Child Went Forth" (1855); each concerns the power of primary imagination to "absorb" (*LG* 248) and preserve in memory, without selection, the riches of the phenomenal world. "Out of the Cradle" is the more ambitious poem, however, for it seeks to place this primary experience of receptivity in the context of its development of a secondary mode, where, "co-existing with the conscious will," perception can attain communicable form. Wordsworth's "Immortality Ode" is an obvious thematic predecessor. Childhood in both "Immortality" and "Out of the Cradle" is viewed as a period of "primal sympathy / Which having been must ever be"; but the child in each poem is helplessly a visionary, a mere medium of receptive consciousness. The opening of "Out of the Cradle" conveys this helplessness in the arbitrariness and intensity of its imagery. The power of things comes from all directions:

> Out of the cradle endlessly rocking,
> Out of the mocking bird's throat, the musical shuttle,
> Out of the Ninth-month midnight,
> Over the sterile sands and the fields beyond, where the child
> leaving his bed wander'd alone, bareheaded, barefoot,
> Down from the shower'd halo,
> Up from the mystic play of shadows twining and twisting
> as if they were alive.   [LG 246–247]

The child in "Out of the Cradle" is liberated from the state of primal sympathy in two stages. The first occurs when, "translating" the bird's lament, the boy suddenly comprehends his own sexuality. The bird, whom he now greets as "brother," has been the "messenger" of "the fire, the sweet hell within" (LG 252). The bird's song has "arous'd" him to awareness of his libido, with all its "unknown want":

> Never more shall I escape, never more the reverberations,
> Never more the cries of unsatisfied love be absent from me,
> Never again leave me to be the peaceful child I was before.
> [LG 252]

What the bird has taught the boy, Whitman says, is the power of song to reveal experience:

Demon or bird! (said the boy's soul,)
Is it indeed toward your mate you sing? or is it really to me?
For I, that was a child, my tongue's use sleeping, now I have
    heard you,
Now in a moment I know what I am for, I awake.

[*LG* 251–252]

The bird's song is beautifully the mirror of his world. In the
magnetic field of the mockingbird's grief, the shifting elements of the moonlit seascape align themselves in images of
loss:

Soothe! soothe! soothe!
Close on its wave soothes the wave behind,
And again another behind embracing and lapping, every one
    close,
But my love soothes not me, not me.   [*LG* 249]

The style of expression Whitman attributes to the bird, however—heavily repetitious and almost exclusively present-tense
—represents a lower order of imagination than the boy will
achieve when he becomes a bard. This is the second recognition the poem records, the second stage of liberation. The boy
intuits that when he has learned to sing *him*self, his songs will
be "clearer, louder and more sorrowful than yours." The cry
the poet looses to the night upon making this judgment—"O
if I am to have so much, let me have more!" (*LG* 252)—can
be viewed as an act of criticism; now that the boy knows love
as loss, his aroused heart wants—unlike the bird's—to know
why. And now because he has been brought by these encounters to an awareness higher than a child's, he is able to
hear the other voice that has been whispering the secret all
along.

The intrusion of the idea of death completes in Whitman's
myth the essential education of the poet: that "it must change"

(*CP* 389) is the very condition of the life of the imagination. Discussing "Song of Myself" above, I observed that the poet was there discovering the boundless diversity of his own imagination; no matter how far out or in deep he went he found only "the depth and height reflecting my own face" (*LG* 46). He could in 1855 easily absorb the fact, as he put it in "Scented Herbage of my Breast," that love and death were "folded inseparably together" (*LG* 115). But in 1860 Whitman's mind had changed its orientations. Stephen Whicher suggests that by that date Whitman had "seen through the Emersonian illusion that the power of the poet prophesies a victory for the man. Whereas 'Song of Myself' had dramatized the omnipotence of bardic vision, 'Out of the Cradle' dramatizes the discovery that the power of the bard is only to sing his own limits."[6]

Death, or limitation, is present in "Out of the Cradle" in two ways: as the condition of the poem, established in the seventy-two lines of its opening that frame the reminiscence; and as a persona in the character of the sea. The one operates as a tension on the other; a boy is dramatized, but a man is giving the scenes their meaning. Hence the sea as a maternal persona is not so frightening as she is for the man in the other poem from this period—"As I Ebb'd with the Ocean of Life" —in which she plays the same role. This is to be the child's first premonition of what Hopkins in "Spring and Fall" called "the blight man was born for," and Whitman offers it to the boy with the same gentleness he shows in a later poem, "On the Beach, at Night," which will bear comparison with this scene at the end of "Out of the Cradle."

"On the Beach" is usually read as a poem about the im-

---

[6] Whicher, "Whitman's Awakening to Death," in *The Presence of Walt Whitman*, ed. R. W. B. Lewis (New York: Columbia University Press, 1962), p. 26.

mortality of the soul, on the assumption that it shares with the other poems of its period (1871) the idea of the soul's transcendence expressed in "Passage to India." But the soul is never mentioned in the "On the Beach"; and the kinds of immortality projected are so alien to human consciousness—the immortality of "vast suns" and "long-enduring pensive moons" (*LG* 259)—that human identity is denied in their symbolism. Moreover, by drawing these symbols into the context of the weeping child clinging to her father's hand, Whitman emphasizes the profound sadness that accompanies a child's first inklings about death, a sadness that the adult's consolatory explanations can rarely vanquish. The child in "On the Beach at Night" weeps like Hopkins' Margaret in a similar poem, because she is possessed by an awful intuition about something beyond her understanding. As Hopkins puts it: "Nor mouth had, nor mind, expressed / What heart heard of" ("Spring and Fall"). Whitman's tactic in dealing with the child's dread is different from Hopkins' gently devastating "It is Margaret you mourn for," since Whitman intends to comfort the child as well as to provide her mind with "the first suggestion, the problem." So Whitman refuses to name that

> Something there is more immortal even than the stars,
> (Many the burials, many the days and nights, passing away,)
> Something that shall endure longer even than lustrous Jupiter,
> Longer than sun or any revolving satellite
> Or the radiant sisters the Pleiades.   [*LG* 259]

The conclusion can be drawn that the child's soul is "more immortal." But here as in "Out of the Cradle" we are on the beach at night, confronting the shifting forms of reality in whose continual change lie both the imagination's wealth and the man's mortality. So I am more inclined to find in the undescribed presence of the sea the correspondence for the "something" that endures. The sea says "death," and of death Whitman says in another poem concerning the mutable world:

> you will perhaps dissipate this entire show of appearance,
> [And] may-be you are what it is all for, but it does not last so very long,
> But you will last very long.   ["Scented Herbage," *LG* 115]

"Out of the Cradle" breathes the same truth, equally tempered to the lamb, through the maternal sea whose voice is sweet and low. I have remarked before on the importance to Whitman of the idea of being "face to face," so it seems significant that while she whispers her word the sea is "bending aside" her old crone's face, while her crone's body is concealed, "swath'd in sweet garments" (*LG* 253). Pronounced as from beneath a veil, the word holds no dread for him, only confirmation that death *is*. The dread will come later, when the poet really "closes" with her in "As I Ebb'd with the Ocean of Life."

The meaning of death is not provided, then, by the drama of encounter between child and sea, but by the poet-narrator who reveals it to be the very ground and condition of the poem. Whitman never went so far as to say, with Wallace Stevens, that "death is the mother of beauty" (*CP* 68), but the organizing metaphor of the rocking cradle and the implications it stirs in the imagery of the opening lines indicate how actively Stevens' principle operated in Whitman's imagination at this time. The lines are delivered with a feeling of urgency. Every image not only involves death with life, but seems to be snatched hastily and anxiously, the poet retrieving what he can from time as it breaks over him like surf:

> From your memories sad brother, from the fitful risings and fallings I heard,

From under that yellow half-moon late-risen and swollen as
   if with tears,
From those beginning notes of yearning and love there in the
   mist,
From the thousand responses of my heart never to cease,
From the myriad thence-arous'd words,
From the word stronger and more delicious than any,
From such as now they start the scene revisiting,
As a flock, twittering, rising, or overhead passing,
Borne hither, ere all eludes me, hurriedly,
A man, yet by these tears a little boy again,
Throwing myself on the sand, confronting the waves,
I, chanter of pains and joys, uniter of here and hereafter,
Taking all hints to use them, but swiftly leaping beyond
   them,
A reminiscence sing.   [LG 247]

Because of his anxiety the speaker is indifferent to rhetorical
logic; the syntax approaches incoherence. This technique of
speech conveys the poet's fear that the poem will not get
written at all, since reminiscences assail and evade him "as a
flock, twittering, rising, or overhead passing"; he must find
their correspondences in language "ere all eludes me." The
significance of the bird's song and the sea's word, then, focus
in this experience of memory's assault on the poet who has
returned as a full-grown bard to the shores where his vocation
was first revealed. From the bird's song he had learned, as he
wrote earlier in "Starting from Paumanok,"

      that what he really sang for was not there only,
   Nor for his mate nor himself only, nor all sent back by the
      echoes,
   But subtle, clandestine, away beyond,
   A charge transmitted and gift occult for those being born.
                                            [LG 22]

Yet the key to even "the sweetest song," the sea has taught

him, is death. The tears he sheds belong to the world of the poem, dying as it is born, and to the condition of the poet, singing as the night deepens, "in the predicate," as Wallace Stevens said, "that there is nothing else" (*CP* 527).

"*When Lilacs Last in the Dooryard Bloom'd*"

Throughout this chapter I have been selecting for study those poems published in 1855, 1856, and 1860 in which Whitman deals with the "path between reality and the soul," and in which he demonstrates the imagination's power to make reality yield a human meaning. As I have remarked with reference to "Song of Myself," Whitman, like Coleridge, appears to distinguish in this activity two distinct phases. The first is a phase of perception, in which the mind opens to the influence of reality: "I lean and loafe at my ease observing a spear of summer grass" (*LG* 28); "I will go to the bank by the wood and become undisguised and naked" (*LG* 29); "I open my scuttle at night and see the far-sprinkled systems" (*LG* 82). The other phase of the act of mind is, as Coleridge puts it, an activity differing "in the *mode* of its operation"; a form-finding phase in which the imagination produces poetry out of perception as a tree puts forth—and then scatters—its leaves: "Accepting the rough deific sketches to fill out better in myself, bestowing them freely on each man and woman I see" (*LG* 75). Whitman's myth of imagination, the story of the Real Me, traces this action from inception to completion, from both the perspective of the mythic autobiography and the perspective of the instant itself. Most of Whitman's poetry in the first three editions of *Leaves of Grass* concerns the resourcefulness of the imagination, and celebrates the inexhaustibility of subjects the world extends to the Real Me through sight and hearing, smell and taste and touch.

But after 1860, as I have indicated before, Whitman's poetry changed. The most radical change, for my purposes, was the virtual disappearance of the persona of the Real Me as hero of the poet's world and speaker of his poems. Under circumstances investigated, inconclusively, by his biographers, Whitman seems in the years 1859–1860 to have suffered traumatic self-doubt, losing permanently his faith in the authority of the "I" who is hero of the first three editions of *Leaves of Grass*. The edition of 1860, of course, was the volume that introduced "As I Ebb'd with the Ocean of Life" and that ended with "So Long!"—the important poems discussed in the preceding chapter. Whitman seems to be sensing a potential exhaustion of the Real Me, and to be hastening to complete his story "While my pleasure is yet at the full" (*LG* 504). Yet the Real Me had one more chant to deliver, the one of all his poems which comes closest to fulfilling the hope for an American bard Whitman expressed in the preface to *Leaves of Grass*, 1855. That was the elegy for Lincoln, "When Lilacs Last in the Dooryard Bloom'd," written in 1865.

The structure of the poem is rather simple. Section 1 (*LG* 328) is an introduction, establishing the poem's setting. Sections 2–4 assemble the major symbols. In 5–13, the mind moves between the opposed symbols of lilac and star, enlarging their meanings until they begin to touch. Section 14 begins with a vision uniting these two symbols; the delayed song of the thrush is delivered. In 15–16 the poet unites all three symbols in a second vision, and, being done with them, releases them back into nature. The process of the poem moves the poet from sheer emotional expression of grief (section 2), to the dignifying indulgence of grief in ceremony (5–13), to an acknowledgment of death supported by both emotion and intellect (14), to translation of grief into a symbolic context penetrated with understanding (15–16).

The introduction of the symbols at sections 2–4 establishes the poem's problem—the occurrence of death in a context that denies it—and the avenue of its solution. The "powerful western fallen star" (*LG* 329) is not only the dead man but, because he has fallen, is also the correlative for the poet's helpless grief: the "black murk" which hides the star, Lincoln, is also "the harsh surrounding cloud that will not free my soul." Opposed to the darkened star in all details is the lilac, whose every leaf is "a miracle" raised annually from death. The third symbol is the bird whose song is "solitary," gives death an "outlet" into life, and provides the singer with the only notion of deathlessness the poem offers.

At section 5 the poet begins to weave the fictive covering for these symbols, drawing out their meanings. In 5–7 a coffin is conducted, under the aegis of lilacs, through a landscape of growth newly uprisen from "shroud[s] in the dark-brown fields" (*LG* 330), and through cities where private mourning is given expression in solemn public ceremony. Placing his sprig of lilac on the coffin, the poet introduces the meaning of the spring fields—regeneration—into the public ceremony which makes death "sane and sacred," for without the observance of ceremony, grief is close to madness and death obscene. Then at 7 he makes this death a universal death:

> All over bouquets of roses,
> O death, I cover you over with roses and early lilies,
> But mostly and now the lilac that blooms the first,
> Copious I break, I break the sprigs from the bushes,
> With loaded arms I come, pouring for you,
> For you and the coffins all of you O death.   [*LG* 331]

Recognition that the death of one man is the death of all advances the poet a degree out of his powerlessness. But the flowers have been cast, as in "Lycidas," "to interpose a little ease." Acknowledging that he is still deeply influenced by emotion, the poet turns to the star.

The poet knows the meaning of the star's symbolism by hindsight. At first appearance the star had been compelling but ambiguous. It drew the poet near—"something I know not what kept me from sleep" (LG 331)—but he could connect it with nothing human. The poet can now solve the earlier mystery and rightly name the star's meaning; but the line "my soul in its trouble dissatisfied sank" indicates the present as well as the past, for he is still detained in baffled sorrow.

Sections 10–13 return meditation to the lilac as fitting decoration for the tomb, enlarging its reference. Not lilac itself but things for which the lilac may stand are the memorials here: all variations on the theme of lilac in dooryards, imaging the beautiful common things that are the trust of a man's life, and that go on as if death could not be. At the end of section 12 Whitman begins to draw these implications of lilac into the field of the star by placing the image of the "floods of the yellow gold of the gorgeous, indolent, sinking sun, burning, expanding the air" (LG 332) in the context of its cyclic journey:

> Lo, the most excellent sun so calm and haughty,
> The violet and purple morn with just-felt breezes,
> The gentle soft-born measureless light,
> The miracle spreading bathing all, the fulfill'd noon,
> The coming eve delicious, the welcome night and the stars,
> Over my cities shining all, enveloping man and land.
>
> [LG 333]

Reference to the "miracle" which fulfills itself then sinks away is the first accommodation of the symbolism of the star to the symbolism of the lilac. It turns on the implication, as in Milton's invocation in *Paradise Lost*, that light is under-

standing, the inward miracle that spreads through and consolidates the mind as light fulfills the landscape by revealing all
it contains.

At section 14, one of Whitman's most beautifully written
lyric passages, the poet masters his grief with understanding.
He sits amid spring fields in the thick light of closing day—
the landscape of both lilac and star—in what he calls "the
large unconscious scenery of my land," as if he were the only
human consciousness in nature, the eye of the world. In a state
of visionary peacefulness, he accepts death as an overarching
reality, a sky under which all common living is performed:

> I saw the ships how they sail'd,
> And the summer approaching with richness, and the fields all
> busy with labor,
> And the infinite separate houses, how they all went on, each
> with its meals and minutia of daily usages,
> And the streets how their throbbings throbb'd, and the cities
> pent—lo, then and there,
> Falling upon them all and among them all, enveloping me
> with the rest,
> Appear'd the cloud, appear'd the long black trail.   [*LG* 334]

The cloud is that same "harsh surrounding cloud that will not
free my soul." But the poet has been freed from it, now, by
opening his mind without defenses to the thought of mortality:

> And I knew death, its thought, and the sacred knowledge of
> death.   [*LG* 334]

This knowledge liberates Whitman much as comparable
knowledge liberates Wordsworth, in a poem with far-reach-
ing similarities to this: the "Immortality Ode," in which
Wordsworth says

> The clouds that gather round the setting sun
> Do take a sober colouring from an eye
> That hath kept watch o'er man's mortality.

For a landscape yields meaning—"thoughts"—when viewed from the perspective of one of the great laws that underlie it, where before it yielded only a visual splendor without human meaning. The landscape is *made* human through the mediation of what Wordsworth calls "the philosophic mind," wisdom won from the heart's experience:

> Thanks to the human heart by which we live,
> Thanks to its tenderness, its joys, and fears,
> To me the meanest flower that blows can give
> Thoughts that do often lie too deep for tears.

Thoughts too deep for tears are the gift, exactly, of Whitman's vision. The "thought" of death he has had all along: like "cruel hands," it has held the soul powerless. It is the star's meaning, what the star "must have meant" him to know (LG 329), and it still walks close with him (*LG* 334) as his grief nears resolution. But now he has also the "sacred knowledge of death," too deep for grief, sacred because, like ceremony, knowledge liberates fact from the realm of futile emotion.

In the last movement of the poem the poet has withdrawn into a darkness created by the enveloping cloud of his visionary state. He practices here the kind of "eloignment from nature" Coleridge describes as the province of primary imagination: "an inward beholding, having a similar relation to the intelligible or spiritual, as Sense has to the material or phenomenal." He remains until attaining the insight which can unify the contradictory spheres of meaning symbolized by lilac and star. "He merely absents himself a season from her, that his own spirit, which has the same ground with nature, may learn her unspoken language in its main radicals, before he approaches to her endless composition of them." This pattern, as I have remarked before, is described in "Starting from Paumanok" and "Song of Myself," and to some degree also in "Out of the Cradle." In all three poems, during withdrawal from outward sense the poet's consciousness is penetrated by a voice that frees his poetic energy.

The thrush's voice in "Lilacs" is like the valvèd voice of the soul in "Song of Myself" and the mockingbird's song in "Out of the Cradle," in that the poet's mind is ravished by it. Issuing from the dark, the bird's carol becomes the voice of the poet's soul, its sacred knowledge that death is a reality *"to all, to each, / Sooner or later"* (*LG* 335); therefore it must be praised along with the rest of the "fathomless universe." But the bird's song goes further in its praise than the poet's grieving mind alone would have taken him. The bird speaks of death as a "deliveress" to whom soul and body in their time willingly turn.

With this insight—essentially the insight of the boy in "Out of the Cradle," and rendered in similar imagery—"Lilacs" moves to its resolution. The song becomes a third element in the poet's mind, together with the thought of death and the knowledge of death, "my comrades there." In their presence

> my sight that was bound in my eyes unclosed,
> As to long panoramas of visions.
>
> And I saw askant the armies,
> I saw as in noiseless dreams hundreds of battle-flags,
> Borne through the smoke of the battles and pierc'd with missiles I saw them,
> And carried hither and yon through the smoke, and torn and bloody,
> And at last but a few shreds left on the staffs, (and all in silence,)
> And the staffs all splinter'd and broken.

I saw battle-corpses, myriads of them,
And the white skeletons of young men, I saw them,
I saw the debris and debris of all the slain soldiers of the war.
                                                [*LG* 336]

The vision unites the contradictory elements in the poet's
mind: the thought of death with its bloody horrors and out-
rages on which the heart looks with pity and fear; and the
knowledge of death, enlarged by the bird's song of praise,
that says these horrors

        were not as was thought,
They themselves were fully at rest, they suffer'd not,
The living remain'd and suffer'd, the mother suffer'd,
And the wife and the child and the musing comrade suffer'd,
And the armies that remain'd suffer'd.   [*LG* 336]

With war and defeat as the vehicles of his meaning, Whitman justifies the bird's otherwise simplistic praise of death as
a deliveress. The skeletons and corpses of young men left like
debris in the American fields are recipients of the lilac broken
at section 7 for all deaths, and are included in the poet's vast
grief over the Civil War, climaxed in Lincoln's assassination.
The young men—and Lincoln too—have been released from
consciousness: this is the ironic "bliss" of death, which of
course can only be known from the perspective of life. Yet
nothing of death's reality to the living is denied in Whitman's
vision, for the musing comrade must still suffer—now, and
again with every returning spring, as the opening of the poem
tells us. Nonetheless, the soul has been liberated from its powerlessness by this vision, for death has yielded up its meanings
under what Wallace Stevens describes as

                        savage scrutiny,
Once to make [its object] captive, once to subjugate
Or yield to subjugation, once to proclaim

The meaning of the capture, this hard prize
Fully made, fully apparent, fully found.   [*CP* 376]

The token of the imagination's release from its subjugation to
the object, death, is its release of the poem's symbols. Lilac,
star, and bird are allowed now to sink back into nature because their meanings have been "tallied" in the poem: "each
to keep and all, retrievements out of the night, . . . twined
with the chant of my soul" (*LG* 337).

Confidence in the brooding mind's power to make even the
most forbidding and forbidden aspects of reality become intelligible and humanly endurable appears for the last time in
Leaves of Grass with the elegy for Lincoln. And this is appropriate, considering Whitman's lifelong ambition to be the
poet of American reality. For the ambition was lifelong; but
Whitman early acknowledged that the inspiration he felt
writing the first three volumes deserted him afterward, never
to return.[7] Yet Whitman seems to have been content that in
the canon of the Real Me he had projected a figure of human
worthiness commensurate with the needs of his nation for its
own mythic hero. On the subject of his sense of accomplish-
ment we may allow Whitman the last words, written early
in 1865 to his friend William O'Connor: "I am satisfied with
Leaves of Grass (by far the most of it) as expressing what
was intended, namely, to express by sharp-cut self assertion,
One's Self, & also, or may be still more, to map out, to throw
together for American use, a gigantic embryo or skeleton of
Personality, fit for the West, for native models."[8]

---

[7] The editors of *Leaves of Grass, Comprehensive Reader's Edition*
quote Whitman to this effect, without citing the source: " 'I do not
suppose,' he said, 'that I shall ever again have the *afflatus* I had in
writing the first *Leaves of Grass*,' and he spoke of his experiment as
a radical utterance out of the abysms of the Soul." See "Introduction," p. xxvii.

[8] *The Correspondence*, ed. Miller, 1, 247.

Chapter 3

Stevens' Muse:
The One of Fictive Music

While, of course, I come down from the past, the past is my own and not something marked Coleridge, Wordsworth, etc. I know of no one who has been particularly important to me. My reality-imagination complex is entirely my own even though I see it in others.

—Wallace Stevens, *Letters*

Like Walt Whitman, Wallace Stevens was reluctant to view himself from the academic point of view which seeks to understand poetry by placing it in a context of influences, sources, and analogues. Yet, as Marius Bewley observed in an article written shortly after Stevens published *Transport to Summer* (1947), "the part of Stevens' meaning which is poetically significant declares him to be an exponent of Coleridge's theory of the imagination."[1] Both Stevens' statement and Bewley's, though contradictory, are true. In the following pages I have attempted a stereoscopic view which takes Coleridge's theory as one source of light and Stevens' imagery as the other. To do so, I hope, is not to ignore Stevens' originality, but rather to bring into focus certain features of Stevens' mythology of imagination, in order to contemplate its resemblance to Whitman's.

The very magnitude of the theme of imagination in Ste-

[1] Bewley, "The Poetry of Wallace Stevens," in *The Achievement of Wallace Stevens* (Philadelphia: Lippincott, 1962), ed. Ashley Brown and Robert S. Haller, pp. 153–154.

vens creates a problem for his interpreter. Whitman's concept of poetic imagination could be discussed in terms of its place in Whitman's mythic autobiography, for imagination in *Leaves of Grass* is a character: the Real Me, the consistently personified aspect of the poet's mind that contains his creative power. Although Whitman's notion of the imagination appears to derive from Emerson's essays on the Over Soul, Whitman did not concern himself much with theories. For Stevens, on the other hand, the imagination was a subject in itself, one he studied from every perspective throughout his life. His ideas about it are often invisibly present as assumptions shaping a poem.

The problem relevant to this discussion, however, is not the whole of Stevens' theory of imagination, but rather that theory when it takes a specific form, comparable to Whitman's, within the poetry—when imagination appears as "an abstraction blooded as a man" (*CP* 385) or woman. Defining the imagination, Stevens variously calls it the power of resisting reality[2] and the process of agreeing with reality;[3] in either definition the imagination is the energy, or active part, of an intelligence which includes the whole personality. In his poetry, Stevens, like Whitman, consistently characterized that mental energy as one or another of several personae. Describing the character types in which Stevens embodies the imagination, however, necessitates describing the evolution of Stevens' thought on the subject of poetic imagination. It is possible to treat Whitman's relations with the Real Me as episodes in an autobiographical narrative. Whitman exhausted this subject within the relatively short span of years between the creation of the first and the third editions of *Leaves of Grass*. Stevens' accounts of poetic imagination extend from

2 "The Noble Rider and the Sound of Words," *NA* 22–23, 27, 36.
3 "The Figure of the Youth as Virile Poet," *NA* 57–59.

his first book, *Harmonium*, to the last poems he wrote before death: "Of Mere Being" and "A Mythology Reflects Its Region" (*OP* 117–118); and the first poems can be read as overtures to all that follow, announcing their major themes and emphases. Yet the later poems explore these themes with a sensibility made more subtle and humane—Stevens would have said more "central"—by years of meditation on the nature of the creative process.

For the sake of organizing what Stevens preferred to treat unsystematically, I shall divide my discussion of Stevens into two chapters, beginning with the characterization of the muse in Stevens, counterpart to what Whitman called the "soul." The major poems in which this persona appear are "It Must Give Pleasure" (from *Notes toward a Supreme Fiction*) and "The Owl in the Sarcophagus." But these long poems cannot easily be discussed without detailed glosses on the persona herself. She is a direct aspect of Stevens' own mind, the receptive mode of consciousness which lends itself to projection in terms of female imagery. She is also the incarnate form of the ideal poem, the supreme fiction, and as such was courted with awe and love by Stevens all his life. He began to develop her symbolism in one of the earliest poems of *Harmonium*.

"To the One of Fictive Music"

Harmonium was the work of a mature man, published like the first *Leaves of Grass* when its author was entering middle age. Stevens was also then a mature poet; the style he displayed in his first book was the work of an impeccable craftsman both of free verse and of blank verse. It has been argued that to a significant degree in *Harmonium*, style *is* the subject,[4] and to the extent that this is true the poems of *Har-*

[4] See Joseph N. Riddel, *The Clairvoyant Eye: The Poetry and*

monium are difficult to assess. The language is often ornate and parodic, and is frequently spoken through a mask (as, for example, in "Le Monocle de Mon Oncle" and "The Weeping Burgher").

"To the One of Fictive Music" presents the reader with several of these characteristic difficulties. Stevens uses an elliptical method of exposition which obscures the poem's argument; the creation of an elevated mood and a brilliant verbal surface imitative of music seem to have been considerations as important as clarity of meaning. Since the poem's argument is my chief concern here, I will approach the poem through terms culled from Stevens' essay "The Figure of the Youth as Virile Poet," where the ideas informing "To the One of Fictive Music" are restated and interpreted.

In the relevant part of this essay Stevens recounts an imaginary history. Out of the seventeenth century, the "time when the incredible suffered most at the hands of the credible," there emerges the first heroic figure "possible," in Stevens' special sense, for modern man. He is seen "stepping forward in the company of a muse of [his] own, [who is] still half-beast and somehow more than human, a kind of sister of the Minotaur." This pair of figures represents "the clear intelligence of the young man still bearing the burden of the obscurities of the intelligence of the old" (*NA* 52–53). The young man's relief from that burden—Stevens calls it a "purification" (*NA* 60)—is accomplished in an act of imagination which brings his whole personality into a relation with reality which is comparable, Stevens says, to the relation between objects and light. "Like light, [imagination] adds nothing but itself" (*NA* 61); it is "a victory over the incredible" (*NA* 53). The act of imagination also performs a liberation of the

Poetics of Wallace Stevens (Baton Rouge: Louisiana State University Press, 1962), pp. 52–53, 284n.

mind tantamount to "the establishing of a self" (*NA* 50): the existence of reality and the self are confirmed and exalted. The youth's response to this moment of "central purity" is to deny the muse as an intelligence necessary to poetic truth-fulness: "No longer do I believe that there is a mystic muse, sister of the Minotaur. This is another of the monsters I had for nurse, whom I have wasted. I am myself a part of what is real, and it is my own speech and the strength of it, this only, that I hear or ever shall" (*NA* 60).

The first part of this story, then, has established the idea of the radical poet as a realist stationed at the center of reality where the pressure is greatest. The second part concerns his virility, his power to press back. In the poet's virility lies his heroism as a cultural figure, for if he is a serious artist, Stevens claims, "the consciousness of his function . . . is a measure of his obligation. . . . Can we think he will elect anything except to exercise his power to the full and at its height, . . . to make his own imagination that of those who have none, or little?" (*NA* 63, 62). The imagination of this central man becomes that of his countrymen, of course, through the medium of his poem, his "imagination of life." Coming as it does from the center of reality it is a "speaking" likeness—indistinguish-able from reality except for that penetration with human sensibility. But that penetration makes all the difference; it is the "unreal" by which reality is transformed for human ends. Acknowledging this truth, the poet's last words reinstate the muse whose function he has before misinterpreted: "Inexplicable sister of the Minotaur, enigma and mask, although I am part of what is real, hear me and recognize me as part of the unreal. I am the truth but the truth of that imagination of life in which with unfamiliar motion and manner you guide me in those exchanges of speech in which your words are mine, mine yours" (*NA* 67).

"To the One of Fictive Music" makes much the same statement. Like the essay, the poem's form recreates an act of discovery. Beginning with the figure close to her traditional
sources, it ultimately, by a process of qualification, recognizes
that she is essential to a theory of poetry.

At the opening of the poem Stevens draws the widest circle
around his central figure, listing the types of the eternal femi-
nine traditionally associated with poetic inspiration:

> Sister and mother and diviner love,
> And of the sisterhood of the living dead
> Most near, most clear, and of the clearest bloom,
> And of the fragrant mothers the most dear
> And queen, and of diviner love the day
> And flame and summer and sweet fire.   [CP 87]

Mingled here are suggestions of the medieval worship of the
Virgin as patroness of the arts and of the Renaissance worship
of her human counterpart in, for example, Beatrice or Laura.
Each is equally of "the sisterhood of the living dead": each
a figure out of an "old intelligence," but Stevens, the modern
realist, strips her in the final lines of her anachronistic costum-
ing. Diction and syntax also grow less euphuistic as—in the
words of the essay—the speaker steps forward out of "the
burden of the obscurities" (NA 53) of his imaginative fore-
bears:

> no thread
> Of cloudy silver sprinkles in your gown
> Its venom of renown, and on your head
> No crown is simpler than the simple hair.   [CP 87]

In stanza two the style becomes meditative, in token, perhaps, of a fuller commitment of the speaker's own intelligence
to the creation of the image:

Now, of the music summoned by the birth
That separates us from the wind and sea,
Yet leaves us in them, until earth becomes,
By being so much of the things we are,
Gross effigy and simulacrum, none
Gives motion to perfection more serene
Than yours, out of our imperfections wrought,
Most rare, or ever of more kindred air
In the laborious weaving that you wear.

The stanza turns on an implied definition of music as "imaginative life," to use the essay's term: life in motion within the imagination. Music is the best synonym for imaginative reality because of all artistic media it is most involved with time—motion—and least dependent on space. Making particularly brilliant use of the intellectual commonplace that the birth of human consciousness was a "fall" away from unity with nature, Stevens evolves a complex metaphorical structure in which wind and sea are at once particulars of reality and names for the perfect music of this ideal figure. The poet is not asking for a miracle of divine intervention, the poetic "fit" ridiculed in Plato's *Ion;* music itself has been created out of the division between mind and reality, so nothing from beyond reality could be of any use in its making. Nor is reality—"earth"—responsible if the mind can fashion only crude images of it. Clearly what is needed is more and better mind. In "The Figure of the Youth as Virile Poet" Stevens does not hesitate to call the possible poet a genius, one who "accumulates experiences and qualities of experience accessible only in the extreme ranges of sensibility" (*NA* 66). Here, echoing the argument of "Sunday Morning" that paradise is only the *idea* made of the earth, he says that perfect music is "of our imperfections wrought." The intelligence which sets such music in motion may be more serene and most rare, yet it is kindred, "sister and mother," to his own. Therefore, if the muse sings at all, her music must resemble that of the singer in "The Idea of Order at Key West" (*CP* 129), a poem which may be read as an extension into greater poetry of the implications of this stanza. In that poem, a "laborious weaving" before the onlooker's eyes gives motion to a perfection, a world in which a chaos, "meaningless plunges of water and the wind," has been "measured" and "portioned out." It is not that the breach between the mind and wind and sea has been closed: the sea throughout remains distinct from the song, making "constant cry . . . inhuman" of its own; it is "merely a place by which she walked to sing." Nor has the singer entered into a transcendentalist's communion with nature, for what she sang was not necessarily what she heard; rather, "She was the single artificer of the world / In which she sang." And in that making the sea becomes no gross effigy of itself, but something wholly new: "Whatever self it had, became the self / That was her song" (*CP* 129). That is what the One of Fictive Music accomplishes in her music "of more kindred air."

The third stanza may be compared with the poet's rejection in the essay of a *mystic* muse; it elaborates further the idea that the perfect poem is the poem of earth, created by a self centered in the real:

> For so retentive of themselves are men
> That music is intensest which proclaims
> The near, the clear, and vaunts the clearest bloom.   [*CP* 88]

A man's mind is as long as his memory, as deep as his thought, and as wide as his perception; but it is limited to these. The highest order of art therefore reproduces "things as they are" (*NA* 25) seen close up, near and clear. It is "a victory over the incredible." Also, as Stevens says in the same place, it es-

tablishes a self, conveying one's identity into reality; as sunlight picks out and warms an object and is thereby known as
a presence, the mind is felt as a presence in the image it creates. The ultimate limitations of the mind are therefore not
conceived in the poem as particularly limiting, when all its
resources of *feeling* can be brought to bear in its encounter
with reality. This is the particular talent of the possible poet
as opposed to the philosopher, who can only press on reality
through his faculty of reason (*NA* 41–43). Describing the
image given motion in such an encounter between poet and
reality, Whitman said "This [is] the far-off depth and height
reflecting my own face" (*LG* 46). Stevens' version is that

> so retentive of themselves are men
>
> . . . . .
>
> [That] of all vigils musing the obscure,
> That apprehends the most which sees and names,
> As in your name, an image that is sure,
>
> . . . . .
>
> in whom
> We give ourselves our likest issuance.   [*CP* 88]

In the act of imagination the neutral alliance between mind
and nature is transformed into something felt as a unity; the
world becomes an object of love, something dear because like
oneself, "my fellow, my self, / Sister and solace, brother and
delight" (*CP* 392).

The One of Fictive Music has so far been viewed in the
poem from three perspectives: as a personified abstraction
termed "poetic inspiration"; as an unpersonified intelligence
capable of informing reality; and as an imaginative artifact—
a name, or an image such as a "bough" or "bush" or "scented
vine"—composed equally of reality and mind. The fourth
stanza presents the subject as a *presence in the mind or in the*

object it creates which has the power of transforming what it encounters:

> Yet not too like, yet not so like to be
> Too near, too clear, saving a little to endow
> Our feigning with the strange unlike, whence springs
> The difference that heavenly pity brings.
> For this, musician, in your girdle fixed
> Bear other perfumes. On your pale head wear
> A band entwining, set with fatal stones.
> Unreal, give back to us what once you gave:
> The imagination that we spurned and crave.

An act of imagination, here called "feigning," involves the mediation of reality by consciousness. The resulting image then contains an "unreal," an element that was not in the object or situation the poet looked at and would not necessarily be there if he looked again. Describing this activity in one mood Stevens calls it "fidgeting" (*CP* 352, 372). But when he is thinking of it as the vocation of the possible poet—like Emerson's scholar, the man whose lifework is to exercise his mind —he calls it "transforming" and attributes to it, as we have seen in the essay, a saving grace. This valuable effect of imagination is seen operating toward the end of "The Idea of Order at Key West." Liberated into the imaginative life of the song, the speaker turns to the landscape and finds it changed:

> the glassy lights,
> The lights in the fishing boats at anchor there,
> As the night descended, tilting in the air,
> Mastered the night and portioned out the sea,
> Fixing emblazoned zones and fiery poles,
> Arranging, deepening, enchanting night.   [*CP* 130]

The unreal which is the origin of "the difference that heavenly pity brings" is not fantastic or abnormal, nor is it the sensibility of a Rimbaud as opposed to the sensibility of a Robert Frost. Rather, it is a gratifying resource accessible only in an artifact of imagination. "To describe it by exaggerating," Stevens says, "[the poet or reader] shares the transformation, not to say the apotheosis, accomplished by the poem. It must be this experience that makes him think of poetry as possibly a phase of metaphysics" (*NA* 49). The difference that heavenly pity brings, then, is the experience of the imaginative life of the poem as a *value:* "The freshness of transformation [that is] the freshness of a world, . . . the freshness of ourselves" (*CP* 397).

Some critics have viewed Stevens' reverent emphasis on the value of imagination as resulting from a nostalgia for Christianity. But I think it is difficult to establish from evidence in the poetry that Stevens felt disinherited or endangered by a godless reality, or that he ever experienced the existentialist's nausea or despair.[5] Stevens' imagination seems to me thoroughly post-Victorian: he does not accept things as they are with the feeling that they are not so good as they were. He seems rather to share the peculiarly American temperament described by R. W. B. Lewis in *The American Adam*, the turn of mind which views the everyday man as "a figure of heroic innocence and vast potentialities, poised at the start of a new history."[6] This is not Stevens' rhetoric, but it is very much his spirit. Even in the world-weary late poems there lingers something of the flavor of Whitman's exclamation in "Starting From Paumanok": "This then is life . . . / How

[5] The view of Stevens as disinherited from Christianity, or as an existentialist with the courage of his despair, are views strongly urged, though in different ways, by J. Hillis Miller in *Poets of Reality* (Cambridge: Atheneum, 1965), pp. 217–223, and by Riddel in *The Clairvoyant Eye*, pp. 269–278.

[6] Lewis, *The American Adam* (Chicago: University of Chicago Press, 1955), p. 1.

curious! how real!" (*LG* 16); the very last lines in Stevens' *Collected Poems* liken hearing the "scrawny cry" of a bird in March to "a new knowledge of reality" (*CP* 534). "To the One of Fictive Music" is a meditation on that kind of grateful awakening, into knowledge of the reality of the "unreal." Rhetorically ornate, it is nonetheless the thoughtful beginning of Stevens' effort to establish for the poetic imagination an imposing persona, one which even a realist could affirm.

"*It Must Give Pleasure*"

Notes toward a Supreme Fiction is Stevens' most ambitious poem about the imagination. But it is the poem most difficult to discuss convincingly because it defies so many of the generalizations with which the critic always wants to begin, while encouraging them with its playfully impressive title, the apparent logicality of its tripartite division, and the stringencies of its form (ten stanzas of seven tercets to each part). It is long and concerns a hero, but it is not an epic; it is about the poet but it is not an autobiography. The poem, in short, transcends generic categories and has no easily identified method of organization. Its form might best be described as "a secondary imitation of thought,"[7] that is, a representation of a mind in the process of describing a poem. The subject is in this case *the* poem: a supreme fiction, or the possible creation of a possible poet. Stevens' *Notes*, the smaller poems of which the larger is composed, are not represented as the supreme fiction itself, but rather as enumerations with illustrations of the requirements a supreme fiction must meet.

The three divisions of the poem, then, correspond to three

[7] Northrop Frye's phrase for this technique in "The Realistic Oriole," in *Wallace Stevens: A Collection of Critical Essays,* ed. Marie Borroff (Englewood Cliffs: Prentice-Hall, 1963), p. 141.

demands Stevens makes upon the possible poem. It must be
abstract—that is, founded upon clear and distinct ideas; it must
change, proving its continual adequacy to a reality shaped by
time; and it must give pleasure. Each of these requirements
is set as a title over a separate poem of ten cantos within the
larger fictive body of *Notes*. As Joseph Riddel has observed,
these three poems have similar structures: "The first three
[cantos of each] sketch out the basic problem, the fourth derives a major proposition, and the next five advance negative
and positive variations leading toward a synthetic conclusion
in the final canto."[8] There is also a larger organizing principle
to each part: to the demand made in each subtitle, the poem
offers a symbolism which provides a framework of imagery
capable of realizing and answering that demand. To the demand that the supreme fiction must be abstract the poem offers the symbol of the sun conceived as "heroic power." The
first part of *Notes* is dominated by the implications of Stevens'
statement in *The Necessary Angel* that the imagination is like
light (*NA* 61); yet, like the sun, the abstract hero of this part
cannot be looked at directly. To meet the demand that the
supreme fiction must change, Stevens musters a collection of
culturally fixed symbols and relaxes their gestures into new
configurations; its central symbol is the statue, but the statue
interpreted as including presidential proclamations, effigies of
seraphs, women in sentimental attitudes, birds and bees, and
several varieties of identifiably "poetic" symbols. The demand
"it must give pleasure" evokes the symbol Man–and–Woman
as the emblematic formulation in which two things of opposite nature, being comprehensible only in terms of each other,
together make a single idea: in this case, the idea of creative
imagination.

"It Must Give Pleasure," then, may be read as a long love

[8] Riddel, *Clairvoyant Eye*, pp. 166–167.

poem in which the partners are mind and reality. It develops canto by canto between projections of the twofold movement of the creative mind identified by Coleridge as primary and secondary, imaged here as male and female personae. Within this movement Stevens develops an explicit myth which culminates in the scene between the poet and his muse in the last canto. Canto I projects the secondary mode of imagination in "masculine" imagery; in II the perceiving mind is primary and female. Canto III represents the poetic *image* in its male aspect, as a king who must die. Canto IV, an allegory of marriage, celebrates the union of primary and secondary—receptive and aggressive—modalities in the creative mind. Canto V begins to shape these Coleridgean themes into a coherent narrative. Cantos V–VI oppose a man's and a woman's minds as they deal with the same problem. She is made the possible muse, while VII shows him to be an implausible poet. Cantos VIII–IX transfer the poem to the mind of the narrator as a man and as Man, and show him discovering his identity as a credible hero. Canto X unites him with his object: the imagined world addressable as "fat girl . . . my summer, my night."

This description of the poem appears to violate its spirit. Certainly Stevens did not write the allegorical narrative my summary outlines. *Notes* as a whole and in its parts seems rather to be an exalted version of the junk-shop of "Dezembrum" (*CP* 218) or the Blue Guitarist's patchings: a collection of odds and ends that represent the collector's range of interest. Yet the poem has a serious purpose, articulated perhaps most clearly in its epilogue: "How simply the fictive hero becomes the real" (*CP* 408). The fictive hero of *Notes* becomes real as the reader discovers how fully ordered is the poem's world beneath its miscellaneous surface, how fully penetrated by thought.

Discussion of "It Must Give Pleasure" should begin with consideration of the prologue to *Notes:*

> And for what, except for you, do I feel love?
> Do I press the extremest book of the wisest man
> Close to me, hidden in me day and night?
> In the uncertain light of single, certain truth,
> Equal in living changingness to the light
> In which I meet you, in which we sit at rest,
> For a moment in the central of our being,
> The vivid transparence that you bring is peace.   [*CP* 380]

These lines preface the whole of *Notes* but seem most closely to approach the concerns of "It Must Give Pleasure"; in tone and imagery they foreshadow the last canto. As a poem, the prologue conforms to the pattern consistent in Romantic renderings of encounters between poet and muse. The poet represents himself as withdrawn into what Stevens calls "the central mind," where he is "met" by the sense of form. The form-giver here is conceived both as female and as light in the Miltonic sense described before with reference to Whitman: the light of perception that by flooding objects reveals their forms, "creates a fresh universe out of nothingness by adding itself" (*CP* 517). Stevens here identifies such light as the "uncertain"—that is, both changeable and undogmatic— light of accurate perception which must be "equal in living changingness" to the light of the sun, the light "in which I meet you." This special light is like the presence of the soul in Whitman:

> I mind how once we lay such a transparent summer morning,
> How you settled your head athwart my hips and gently
>   turn'd over upon me,
> And parted the shirt from my bosom bone, and plunged your
>   tongue to my bare-stript heart,

> And reach'd till you felt my beard, and reach'd till you held
> my feet.
>
> Swiftly arose and spread around me the peace and knowledge
> that pass all the argument of the earth.   [LG 33]

In Stevens, typically, the intimate meeting is not located in a
space and a season; it is wholly a state of mind and heart. But
the light shed is the same. It gives to reality a "vivid transparence that . . . is peace," and by it the poet can see into the
life of things. The visitation of this light-bearing beloved satisfies temporarily but decisively the poet's longing that "the
real will from its crude compoundings come" (CP 404). It is
reality's response to desire—an effect said by Stevens to be
produced by the imagination but not by the reason (CP 218)
—and for Stevens as for Whitman is addressable metaphorically as a lover: "We plant you permanently within us, / We
fathom you not—we love you" Whitman concludes in "Crossing Brooklyn Ferry" (LG 165); while Stevens asks in the
same mood of ravishment, "And for what, except for you, do
I feel love?"

The exalted love felt for a world that answers the imagination's need is the ultimate kind of pleasure the supreme fiction
can yield, as the last canto of the poem will say again. Mean-
while, to justify the mythic transfiguration of poet and image
into lover and paramour on the ambitious scale undertaken in
"It Must Give Pleasure," a conceptual foundation must be
laid. This is a concern of the first three cantos.

The imagination, according to Stevens, performs two characteristic activities. One, as he has said in "To the One of
Fictive Music," is the projection of an idea of order, an "unreal," onto reality. The other activity is the clearing of "intelligence" from sight, so that reality may be seen "without
evasion by a single metaphor" (CP 373). These are, of course,

really only one activity viewed from two perspectives: viewed in the first case as if the imagination penetrated reality and in the second as if reality penetrated imagination. Both are creative acts of perception, but one is intrusive, the other receptive. Representing them here, Stevens assigns these two activities to separate cantos and differentiates them as functions of a male principle and a female principle within the mind. The poetic mind in canto I (*CP* 398) is male, begetter of images. Stevens reverts perhaps ironically to the sublimities of "Sunday Morning" in describing a ritual celebration by "crested" and "maned" youths chanting in orgy, isolating among them the figure of Jerome, translator of the Psalms and hence a founder of ritual celebration. His motive, "to find of light a music issuing," is admired—it is the motive of *Notes toward a Supreme Fiction*—but re-enactment of ritual is not an act of imagination:

> the difficultest *rigor* is forthwith,
> On the image of what we see, to *catch* from that
>
> Irrational moment its unreasoning,
> As when the sun comes rising.   [italics mine]

Canto II offers an alternative view of the imagination, its receptive aspect, in the figure of a lady who in midsummer—the season emblematic in Stevens of "vividest repose" (*CP* 375)—gazes with the deepest composure upon the plenitude of sensual forms in nature:

> The blue woman, linked and lacquered, at her window
> Did not desire that feathery argentines
> Should be cold silver, neither that frothy clouds
> Should foam, be foamy waves, should move like them,
> Nor that the sexual blossoms should repose
> Without their fierce addictions.

The lady is all eye, the perceiving organ which connects the present with memory, the faculty of mind most closely associated with the classical muse. The motion of her imagination is not "catching," as in canto I, but recognizing:

> It was enough for her that she remembered.
> The blue woman looked and from her window named
>
> The corals of the dogwood, cold and clear,
> Cold, coldly delineating, being real,
> Clear and, except for the eye, without intrusion,
>
> [*CP* 399–400]

With canto III (*CP* 400) the focus shifts from imagination to the image it creates.

> A lasting visage in a lasting bush,
> A face of stone in an unending red,
> Red-emerald, red-slitted-blue, a face of slate,
>
> An ancient forehead hung with heavy hair.   [*CP* 400]

The male effigy represents a dying order of religion—that is, the body of social values transmitted in imaginative form—about to be overthrown by a new dispensation, symbolized as an orphic shepherd. Religion springs from the deepest impulses of imagination, but tends to petrify into fixed forms, which are then preserved in culture so long that their authority becomes a subjugating rather than a liberating influence on the individual imagination. This idea is represented in the material of which each figure is composed. The cornelian effigy (Stevens is perhaps punning on the derivation of the stone's name from *caro*, the Latin for "flesh") is heavy with ancientness, tedium, and renown, as well as with the weight of stone, whereas the bodiless shepherd's form is sensual music. The two figures are richly invested with the implications of the first two commandments of *Notes*—it must be abstract and it must change—but here the important issue is their power to give pleasure. The ancient statue, like an impotent king, represents the exhaustion of one line of the imagination: he must dominate by oppression. The shepherd who slays him for the poem restores freedom and fertility to the kingdom:

> Children in love . . . brought early flowers
> And scattered them about, no two alike.   [*CP* 400]

The opening lines of canto IV refer directly back to the assertion in canto I that the most rigorous act of imagination is to "catch from the irrational moment its unreasoning." Thought is an aspect of imagination, but in an act of imagination it follows on perception and operates not as reason alone, but in cooperation with the will, in order to "make" something of perception:

> We reason of these things with later reason
> And we make of what we see, what we see clearly
> And have seen, a place dependent on ourselves.   [*CP* 401]

Thus the transaction between imagination and reality depends upon a disciplined passivity as well as a rigorous activity within the mind itself; when these are present in the right degree, reality yields to the mind and becomes fully known.

This statement of an epistemology by now familiar in Stevens prefaces in canto IV a parable concerning a wedding of the right people in the right place at the right time. It is one of the most successful poems in *Notes*. Much of its appealing mixture of lightness and tenderness is due to a managing of rhythm. As in "To the One of Fictive Music," the lines wind into rhyme at various points of internal caesura. The unexpected rhyming and the repetitive formula of the ceremonial hymn create an effect both sublime and parodic of the sublime:

> This was their ceremonial hymn: Anon
> We loved but would no marriage make. Anon
> The one refused the other one to take,
>
> Foreswore the sipping of the marriage wine.
> Each must the other take not for his high,
> His puissant front nor for her subtle sound,
>
> The shoo-shoo-shoo of secret cymbals round.   [CP 401]

The time of the marriage is noon on the first of July. The place, "Catawba," has the name of an Indian tribe of South Carolina, an allusion extended in the poem's evocation of the story of Captain John Smith and the maiden Pocahantas. Both the time and the place have significance that reaches deep into Stevens' complex myth of the seasons. "Credences of Summer," a poem from this same volume, proposed summer as a name for reality's intensity experienced by a mind that has laid by its trouble (CP 372) and is at rest within a state of joyful self-esteem. The summer-seeming mind is in love with reality, but like any lover is not always successful in either pursuit or surrender—a fact of life acknowledged in the marriage hymn: "Anon / We loved but would no marriage make." But occasionally comes an instant when reality fills the poised sensibility to the brim. The seasonal analogy is midsummer noon, described in the meditations of "Credences" as an instant when

> Things stop in that direction and since they stop
> The direction stops and we accept what is
> As good. The utmost must be good and is
> And is our fortune and honey hived in the trees
> And mingling of colors at a festival.   [CP 374]

This "utmost" becomes a place in time, "a place dependent on ourselves," and when it is a summer—as opposed to spring, autumn or winter—place, it is thought of as

the natural tower of all the world,
The point of survey, green's green apogee,
But a tower more precious than the view beyond,
A point of survey squatting like a throne,
Axis of everything, green's apogee

And happiest folk-land, mostly marriage hymns.   [*CP* 373]

The description of the wedding of the personae of summer takes into account all these implications of its symbolic setting. It is a marriage of mind with reality, but each figure represents both a power of mind and a symbolic aspect of reality. The great captain is the principle of imagination defined earlier as secondary, discoverer and creator of forms in reality, and Bawda (body?) is the form he has discovered:

The great captain loved the ever-hill Catawba
And therefore married Bawda, whom he found there.

[*CP* 401]

Bawda is the primary principle of imagination represented earlier in the blue woman's level gaze; the great captain is the presence of reality, that which fills her sight:

And Bawda loved the captain as she loved the sun.

Their marriage is the fusion of these two aspects of imagination in an act of beholding and creating a reality which is a place in time, Bawda its earth, the captain its sun. It is a temporary perfecting of reality within the imagination, the transfiguring of the commonplace in which reality is mastered for the mind by desire and truth, feeling and thought.

With the parable of the marriage in Catawba the fragmentary development of "It Must Give Pleasure" ends, and a narrative carries the poem in one movement to its conclusion. Within the framing symbols of man and woman which give the abstract principles of "It Must Give Pleasure" imaginative

forms, the focus shifts from the nature of the imagination itself to the relation between imagination and the world. The
male factor becomes the virility of imagination, its ability to
master reality; and the female, reality seen as the potential
bride of the imagination.

Stevens, absent as "I" in *Notes* since the dedication, re-
enters the poem at canto V as a persona to be played off
against another persona, the Canon Aspirin, with reference to
a third, the Canon's widowed sister. There is no effort to
maintain dramatic verisimilitude, but these cantos use dramatic
and narrative methods as organizing principles. The Canon
Aspirin is an almost Trollopian creation, a highly civilized and
likable churchman with worldly tastes which, the first lines
suggest, have been supported by aristocracy and Empire. He
tells feelingly the story of a poor relation, his sister, who by
good management and exquisite taste induces "sensible ec-
stacy" out of a context of life that might have meant squalor.
A widow, she lives with her two young daughters according
to a code of extreme propriety which is not at all mean or
unimaginative; rather it resembles the decorum appropriate
to an art:

> She had two daughters, one
> Of four, and one of seven, whom she dressed
> The way a painter of pauvred color paints.
>
> But still she painted them, appropriate to
> Their poverty, a gray-blue yellowed out
> With ribbon, a rigid statement of them, white,
>
> With Sunday pearls, her widow's gayety.   [*CP* 402]

The widow resembles the blue woman of canto II in desiring
only to see things as they are, including her children. She is
also, like the blue woman, sparing of language: she gives her
daughters simple names, "And what she felt for them fought

off the barest phrase." Thinking of her virtues as a woman
and mother, the canon is moved to hum "an outline of a
fugue / Of praise, a conjugation done by choirs." Yet, Stevens concludes:

> when her children slept, his sister herself
> Demanded of sleep, in the excitements of silence
> Only the unmuddled self of sleep, for them.

Within almost any framework of interpretation canto V
establishes the widow as a figure of adequate imagination;
within the framework I have chosen she may be viewed as
primary imagination. But there are details in the canto that
distinguish her from her sisters in "It Must Give Pleasure,"
Bawda and the blue woman. She is not "linked and lacquered"
but poor; she is not married but widowed. Her expectations
center without illusion in her children. The context of Stevens' female symbols in *Notes toward a Supreme Fiction*
permits one to view the widow as the receptive or primary
aspect of imagination, adequate to the realities of an impoverished age, but without a counterpart.

The Canon is more ambiguous. He is a descendant of the
same noble stock as she, but affluent (one gathers from his
luxurious tastes) and wed not to a woman but to an institu-
tion, the church. By this detail and by the implications of his
preferences in music, the Canon is connected with the poem's
critique of ritual celebration, which the first canto has called
"facile exercise" (*CP* 398). The quality of his imagination is
the subject of the next two cantos.

Canto VI recounts the flight of the Canon's imagination
into his central mind, an action that will have transformed
him into an angel by the end of VII. His "eloignment from
Nature" takes place, like the children's, in sleep. Since they
are female children, their sleep is not to be tricked out in

dreams, if their mother's watchfulness can prevent it; but for the Canon, as the male half of imagination, the mental quest must conclude in image-making. The flight itself has two distinct movements delineating again the pattern of an act of imagination, which first peceives, then conceives, "reasons with a later reason." One movement has its destination at the limit of fact: reaching it the Canon focuses on the sight of the children's beds. The other has its destination at the limit of thought, the mental image he will make of what he has seen. That becomes the subject of the next canto, where the Canon is observed imposing orders "as he thinks of them."

> he builds capitols and in their corridors,

> Whiter than wax, sonorous, fame as it is,
> He establishes statues of reasonable men,
> Who surpassed the most literate owl, the most erudite

> Of elephants.   [CP 403]

The images which the Canon, as a modern man, retrieves from his flight represent secular rather than sacred authority. But the statue of a reasonable man, as we know from the rest of the poem, is the direct antithesis of the virile youth who will have to be found for the widow's daughters. The Canon's flight of imagination "is a brave affair" but does not produce the "amassing harmony" he intended.

At this point, approximately a third of the way through VII, the mood of the poem changes. It is as if by meeting up with the Canon, learning of the marvelous sister, seeing how the Canon lived his decent and aspiring life according to the demands of the highest order of imagination he was capable of serving, the narrator had suddenly realized, "Not he, but I am the man." The setting for this breathtaking discovery—conversation at dinner and the retirement of the narrator's

host—is, as I have suggested, only barely dramatic or narrative. But it is enough of both to create mounting intensity in
the mind of the narrator watching the Canon's flight and listening to the music, the imaginative order, the Canon makes
of it. "To impose," the narrator declares suddenly, "is not to
discover":

> To discover an order as of
> A season, to discover summer and know it,
>
> To discover winter and know it well, to find,
> Not to impose, not to have reasoned at all,
> Out of nothing to have come on major weather,
>
> It is possible, possible, possible. It must
> Be possible. It must be that in time
> The real will from its crude compoundings come.
>
> [*CP* 403–404]

The canto ends with an authoritative silencing of the Canon
so that the authentic poet may step forward to speak in canto
VIII:

> Angel,
> Be silent in your luminous cloud and hear
> The luminous melody of proper sound.

The angel of this movement is an alternative (and sexless)
identity of the one of fictive music, the incarnate voice of the
"unreal" which can "give back to us what once [it] gave."
The Canon makes an inauthentic angel because his imagery
derives from inadequate ideas. But because this is a "supreme"
fiction, and because Stevens' imagination is obsessed by Christianity, the angel as icon must be revived, and is, as the poet
recognizes his *own* identity as the authentic voice of the unreal. Thus at line 567 of *Notes toward a Supreme Fiction*, the
first person singular pronoun is spoken for the first time. The

hero ceases there to be a projected persona, such as the "virile youth" of Stevens' essay, and becomes "I." For, unlikely as the comparison may seem, *Notes toward a Supreme Fiction* has an ambition correspondent to the ambition of "Song of Myself": to prove the modern hero to be "any man of imagination," so that when he says "I" he means with Whitman, "It is you talking just as much as myself, I act as the tongue of you, / Tied in your mouth, in mine it begins to be loosen'd" (*LG* 85). Moreover, these final cantos encompass fully as much territory as "Song of Myself." In his poem Whitman ranges from the claim:

> The pleasures of heaven are with me and the pains of hell are with me,
> The first I graft and increase upon myself, the latter I translate into a new tongue.   [*LG* 48]

to the claim:

> a leaf of grass is no less than the journey-work of the stars.
> [*LG* 59]

Stevens at the end of *Notes* appropriates the same boundaries and states the same credos, in his own terms.

The intrusion of the narrator as himself occurs abruptly at the opening of canto VII in a gesture having the effect and tone of cutting through cant, like Whitman suddenly announcing toward the end of "Song of Myself," "It is time to explain myself—let us stand up" (*LG* 80). Stevens' is a question: "What am I to believe?" (*CP* 404). The remaining three cantos answer it. Belief must accommodate both desire and reality, the desire for an absolute and the reality of an ephemeral present. The poet begins, therefore, by imagining an angel, the absolute embodied in human form, and then makes him possible to believe in. The angel will have to be able to make music of the "violent abyss" of the human present, forgetting the "gold centre, the golden destiny" which are the concern, for instance, of Milton's angels. The terms on which this angel is imagined, rather than specific details about him, are the clue to his possibleness. In an earlier poem describing the creation of the poetic image, Stevens described the creative act as an intersection, brought about by the observer's will, between an object, "Projection A," and the contents of the mind, "Projection B," to fetch from the flux of experience an artifact which partakes of both mind and object: "is half who made [it]," and thus "contains the desire of the artist" (*CP* 296). In *Notes* Stevens asks, "If the angel in his cloud . . . / Grows warm in the motionless motion of his flight . . . / Am I that imagine this angel less satisfied? . . . Is it he or is it I that experience this?" (*CP* 404) And the rest of the canto affirms that a man's *experience* of "expressible bliss" makes the symbol of an angel credible:

> Is it I then that keep saying there is an hour
> Filled with expressible bliss, in which I have
>
> No need, am happy, forget need's golden hand,
> Am satisfied without solacing majesty,
> And if there is an hour there is a day,
>
> There is a month, a year, there is a time
> In which majesty is the mirror of the self:
> I have not but I am and as I am, I am.

Moreover, the external regions—the heaven in which the angel is thought to live by the Canon Aspirin—amount simply to the space in which projected human desire is reflected back in anthropomorphic images:

> These external regions, what do we fill them with
> Except reflections, the escapades of death,
> Cinderella fulfilling herself beneath the roof?

Section VII returns the mind from heaven to earth, its proper sphere. The setting is pastoral but makes of nature a garden, wilderness subdued to the civilized human uses of a *fête champêtre*. Stevens enjoins the pleasing racket of the birds from "It Must Change," VI, to celebrate the discovery that men can do all that angels can. The invitation is appropriate because the calling birds seem to express joy in mere being, but the poem works toward the disclosure that pleasure in mere being is a purely human experience. Birds cannot, like men, ever be free of "need's golden hand." The cock robin is a "forced bugler" because his art, Darwin discovered almost sadly, is the gift of a very pragmatic Mother Nature: he whistles for a mate. In addition, the birds have no consciousness of change. Their reality is "an earth in which the first leaf is the tale [i.e., the whole amount, as well as the story] of leaves" (*CP* 394); whereas to a man every leaf is a thing to be brought into the sphere of his consciousness and mastered by thought and feeling, where it may appear, to recall Whitman, "no less than the journey-work of the stars." Thus to enjoy like men—the heroic ideal of the poem—becomes in this canto simply to enjoy as a final good "the way a leaf / Above the table spins its constant spin." Precisely here the narrator locates his virility as a hero:

> Perhaps,
> The man-hero is not the exceptional monster,
> But he that of repetition is most master.   [*CP* 406]

In canto X this heroic power is affirmed in the presence of reality as his paramour.

> Fat girl, terrestrial, my summer, my night,
>
> . . . . .
>
> You remain the more than natural figure. You
> Become the soft-footed phantom, the irrational

Distortion, however fragrant, however dear.
That's it: the more than rational distortion,
The fiction that results from feeling. Yes, that.   [*CP* 406]

Collectively implicated in these lines are the other female
figures of *Notes*—and for that matter, the other "fragrant"
and "dear" ladies of fictive music elsewhere in the *Collected
Poems*. Bawda and the blue woman, because of their associa-
tions with summer and night, might be particularly brought
to the reader's mind, but the poem disallows a narrow reference. As in "To the One of Fictive Music," the "you" addressed includes all possible images of the "unreal" She the
poet loves. The form of canto X is a one-sided dialogue between the poet as lover and reality as his coy mistress, a lady
represented like the angel of "Angel Surrounded by Paysans"
as evasive, a figure "half seen . . . an apparition apparelled
in / Apparels of such lightest look that a turn / Of [her]
shoulder and quickly, too quickly, [she is] gone" (*CP* 497).
The poem opens with a question to her. Since the form the
poet's mind embraces is apprehended as "a moving contour, a
change not quite completed," how is it that he finds the lady
at all? The problem is somehow to locate her essence, "hold
her to herself." The narrator turns on her a realist's eye, attempting to think of her as unenhanced for him by beauty or
responsiveness, as strong, tired, bent over work, anxious, content or alone. But, he discovers, she remains in his mind "the
more than natural figure . . . the irrational distortion." By
this he seems to mean two things: he does not find her because she loves him, and he does not find her by reasoning
about her. The aberrance in her as she is "found" is his own
feeling: she is the fiction—not something found in nature—
"that results from feeling." Stevens' question, "how is it I find
you?" is essentially the same question Whitman addresses to
reality in "Crossing Brooklyn Ferry": "What is it then be-

tween us?" (*LG* 162); and the answer each poem gives is the
same. For each poet, reality perceived sympathetically is reality felt as a presence. "Flood-tide below me," Whitman begins, "I see you face to face!" And further, a world so found
—things indicating what they are—sustains the poet in a certainty of meaning that needs no other authority. The question
"What am I to believe?" has thus been answered too. The
rhetoric of canto X is not Whitman's, but its import is, and
the last canto of *Notes toward a Supreme Fiction* reaffirms
the faith of "Crossing Brooklyn Ferry":

> You have waited, you always wait, you dumb, beautiful
>   ministers,
> We receive you with free sense at last, and are insatiate
>   henceforward,
> Not you any more shall be able to foil us, or withhold your-
>   selves from us,
> We use you, and do not cast you aside—we plant you per-
>   manently within us,
> We fathom you not—we love you—there is perfection in you
>   also,
> You furnish your parts toward eternity,
> Great or small, you furnish your parts toward the soul.
>
> [*LG* 165]

We are not finished with this canto, however, when we
have seen it within the larger achievements of *Notes* as an
American poem, a Romantic poem, and a poem about belief.
It is also the last exploration of the relation between mind and
reality within the symbolic framework established by "It
Must Give Pleasure." Stevens has throughout the nine preceding cantos projected this relation in terms of single personae,
male and female; in terms of a wedding and consummation;
in terms of brave widowhood and benevolent bachelorhood.
At the end he renders it in terms of feelings so intimate and

simple, and of understanding between the partners so profound, that we seem to be overhearing affectionate banter between husband and wife. This canto is appropriate as a conclusion, fulfilling the requirement of *Notes* that the ideal to
be credible must also be commonplace. The very commonplace quality of the language and situation in canto X makes
possible a remarkable effect in the last stanza. Satisfied with
the definition he has found for her, the narrator projects for
his listening spouse his own fanciful version of the apocalypse,
containing echoes of *The Divine Comedy*. Referring again to
the opposition between institutionalized and virile imagination, he tells her that they will know the world has been
delivered from its fallen state the day they hear in a lecture
at the Sorbonne what he has discovered simply through faithfulness to the imagination:

> They will get it straight one day at the Sorbonne.
> We shall return at twilight from the lecture
> Pleased that the irrational is rational,
>
> Until flicked by feeling, in a gildered street,
> I call you by name, my green, my fluent mundo.
> You will have stopped revolving except in crystal.
>
> [CP 406–407]

The city streets in the last light of day have been transformed
by the subtlest touch, a flick of feeling, into the golden streets
of the heavenly city, and the spouse into the divine presence
within the last of the crystalline spheres. Yet this is common
experience for the man of imagination, "he who of repetitions
is most master."

"The Owl in the Sarcophagus"

Stevens attempted the image of the female muse as a personified abstraction of the poet's authority once more on a

grand scale in "The Owl in the Sarcophagus" (*CP* 431), a poem from the volume *The Auroras of Autumn*. "The Owl in the Sarcophagus" may be viewed as counterpart to the third part of *Notes toward a Supreme Fiction* discussed above, its necessary other half. "It Must Give Pleasure" is a love poem which celebrates the light of the unreal as a beloved presence, eternally desired and eternally recoverable. "The Owl in the Sarcophagus" is an elegy (for Henry Church: see *LWS* 566) which contemplates "The *changingness* [of] the light / In which I meet you" (italics mine).

The poem is an effort to write "the mythology of modern death" (*CP* 435). The first section describes the central characters in the myth, identifying three analogical forms in which death has been personified throughout poetic tradition: "high sleep," "high peace," and memory. The second, transitional, section carries the myth into the mind of a grieving man, to test it on the pulses. The poem is completed in four more sections which contemplate and affirm the central symbols of the myth, and finally affirm man's need for the act of mythmaking. In face of death the mind evolves "monsters of elegy" because

> It is a child that sings itself to sleep,
> The mind, among the creatures that it makes,
> The people, those by whom it lives and dies.   [*CP* 436]

"Two forms move among the dead," Stevens begins: "high sleep, / Who by his highness quiets them, high peace, / Upon whose shoulders even the heavens rest" (*CP* 431). These two are visible forms, human figures projected from what the eyes can tell us about the state of death. But there is a third form there too: a woman dimly glimpsed, known, rather, as a "voice that says / Good-by in the darkness, speaking quietly there / To those that cannot say good-by themselves." These mythic forms, Stevens emphasizes, are traditional but not anachronistic ("abortive figures"): neither statues ("rocks") nor supernatural beings ("impenetrable symbols"). Rather, they are abstractions or "first ideas" born of the mind's creative will to make meanings. Sleep and peace are said to be brothers: being human forms, brothers to men, and in their symbolic roles, brothers to each other as well—though "sleep the brother is the father, too, / And peace is cousin by a hundred names" (CP 432). The third figure is known in the words "keep you, I am gone"; she, Stevens says, "is the mother of us all." So far are these forms anthropomorphic and therefore knowable. But, the last line of the first section adds, "the thought of these dark three / Is dark, thought of the forms of dark desire." The mind creates them out of desire for "supremest images, / The pure perfections of parental space" (CP 436), and attributes knowledge to them, but it cannot guess what they know, as children cannot know their parents' thoughts. For the mind has to stop where death begins; it can only deal with death's appearances, its enigmatic resemblances to life, and thus knows death by analogy rather than by experience.

Despite its limitations, the mind can find in its mythologies the kinds of knowledge it needs. This is the subject of the second section:

> one day
> A man walked living among the forms of thought
> To see their lustre truly as it is
>
> And in harmonious prodigy to be,
> A while, conceiving his passage as into a time
>
> . . . . .
>
> Less time than place, less place than thought of place
> And, if of substance, a likeness of the earth,
> That by resemblance twanged him through and through.
>
> [CP 432–433]

The kinds of truth discoverable in these forms of thought are the subject of the next three sections. Sleep and peace, being visible forms which are known through their appearances, are characterized by their costumes. Sleep wears a robe into which all color is absorbed as it strikes, as if his garment were a kind of reverse prism: "unique composure, harshest streakings joined / In a vanishing-vanished violet that wraps round / The giant body the meaning of its folds." Stevens glosses this vanishing of color into whiteness by defining sleep as "ultimate intellect." It is monumental, serene, and perceived as from a distance

> As a moving mountain is, moving through day
> And night, colored from distances, central,
> Where luminous agitations come to rest,
>
> In an ever-changing, calmest unity.   [CP 433]

Sleep, then, symbolizes the collective human mind which majestically survives individual expressions of itself, absorbing even the most contradictory of these into a unity signified by its brilliant whiteness, "A diamond jubilance beyond the fire." Sleep may be compared to the anonymous "thinker of the first idea" of *Notes*, the human power analogous to the merely natural sun. Peace is the carefully designed opposite of this figure, equally imposing but viewed in stroboscopic rather than steady light, representing the inexhaustible diversity of the forms in which "first ideas" are expressed in "a thousand begettings." For peace is the symbol for collective man's creative works, his acts of fancy and imagination:

> Generations of the imagination piled
> In the manner of its stitchings, of its thread,
> In the weaving round the wonder of its need,

And the first flowers upon it, an alphabet
By which to spell out holy doom and end,
A bee for the remembering of happiness.

Peace stood with our last blood adorned, last mind,
Damasked in the originals of green,
A thousand begettings of the broken bold.   [CP 434]

Sleep is father to peace, as perceptions precede and inform images; but peace, being the emblem of our human creativity, is described as the figure that "keeps" us in our death, "a king as candle by our beds, / In a robe that is our glory as he guards" (CP 435).

These figures, then, are Stevens' version of Yeats's symbolic "sages standing in God's holy fire" in Byzantium, monuments of the soul's magnificence. They are conceived as completed, fulfilled, static. The third character in the mythology of the imagination of death, however, is another version of the one of fictive music. She might best be described as Elegy personified. The necessity for the existence of elegy, "death's outlet song" (LG 337), is one of the traditional subjects of the conventional elegy; as Milton, following Theocritus, Moschus, and Virgil, wrote of Lycidas:

> He must not float upon his wat'ry bier
> Unwept, and welter to the parching wind,
> Without the meed of some melodious tear.

The nameless "she" of Stevens' elegy is the embodiment of this motive, "she that says / Good-by in the darkness, speaking quietly there, / To those that cannot say good-by themselves" (CP 431). Further, Stevens emphasizes that she possesses a special kind of knowledge. She

> stood tall in self, not symbol, quick

And potent, an influence felt instead of seen.
She spoke with backward gestures of her hand.
She held men closely with discovery.

. . . . .

It was not her look but a knowledge that she had.
She was a self that knew, an inner thing,
Subtler than look's declaiming, although she moved

With a sad splendor, beyond artifice,
Impassioned by the knowledge that she had,
There on the edges of oblivion.   [CP 435]

Stevens' diction is characteristically abstract, but his emphasis on the passionate energy of her knowledge suggests that she is a personification of the state of urgent imagination Whitman recalls so beautifully in the opening lines of "Out of the Cradle Endlessly Rocking." The power of Whitman's overture derives in part from the sense of mounting tension the reader feels as twenty-one lines accumulate before Whitman provides the main clause of the sentence. Whitman dramatizes in "Out of the Cradle" what I have called the motive toward elegy—the pressure of the mind "on the edge of oblivion" to prevent things it has loved from vanishing entirely in the flux of time: "ere all eludes me." Stevens' symbol, like Whitman's passage, embodies both that motive and its product, the

                    syllable between life

And death [that] cries quickly, in a flash of voice,
Keep you, keep you, I am gone, oh keep you as
My memory.   [CP 432]

She represents the power of language to make what Whitman called "retrievements" of the identities of ephemeral things. In this function she is related to the archetype Mnemosyne: mother of the Muses, hence the origin of aesthetic form. She "is the mother of us all" (*CP* 432) in the sense that acute consciousness of death fosters the consciousness of beauty. As in Whitman, in Wallace Stevens "Death" is the word "which I do not forget,"

> [But fuse] with the thousand responsive songs at random,
> My own songs awaked from that hour,
> And with them the key, the word up from the waves,
> The word of the sweetest song and all songs,
> That strong and delicious word which, creeping to my feet,
> (Or like some old crone rocking the cradle, swathed in sweet
>   garments, bending aside,)
> The sea whisper'd me.   [*LG* 253]

That this figure should be maternal is consistent with Stevens' iconography throughout the *Collected Poems* ("Death is the mother of beauty, mystical . . ." [*CP* 69]). It is especially consistent with the iconography of the volume of *The Auroras of Autumn*, where "the vivid transparence" of creative intelligence is imaged as an ultimate refuge of the aging mind, itself on the edge of oblivion, seeking reaffirmation of its own existential validity:

> The mother's face,
> The purpose of the poem, fills the room.
> They are together, here, and it is warm,
>
> With none of the prescience of oncoming dreams,
> It is evening. The house is evening, half-dissolved.
> Only the half they can never possess remains,
>
> Still-starred. It is the mother they possess,
> Who gives transparence to their present peace.   [*CP* 413]

With this reference to the mother who is both a real memory and a symbol for the "unreal," or grace-dispensing element in poetry, we have come full circle, back to the One of Fictive Music.

> Sister and mother and diviner love,
>
> . . . . .
>
> Unreal, give back to us what once you gave:
> The imagination that we spurned and crave.   [CP 87–88]

It is a linkage that can be discovered only through the artifice of critical analysis. Yet juxtaposing these texts allows a reader to observe how genuinely mythopoeic Stevens' mind was. The history of this female symbol begins with Stevens' contemplation of her as a potentially recoverable icon in poetic tradition, "sisterhood of the living dead." By the final decade he has perfected a style and a confidence commensurate with his ambition. At the end of his life, meditation on "the purpose of the poem" is for Stevens an act which can recover in maturity what Wordsworth called "the primal sympathy": the state of innocent openness which is the beginning of all creative insight, the primary phase of imagination, a condition of holiness wherein the soul's voice again approaches the ear.

> There may always be a time of innocence.
>
> . . . . .
>
>   That we partake thereof,
> Lie down like children in this holiness,
> As if, awake, we lay in the quiet of sleep,
>
> As if the innocent mother sang in the dark
> Of the room and on an accordian, half-heard,
> Created the time and place in which we breathed.
>
>   [CP 418–419]

Chapter 4

The Poet
in the Sun

If we are to think of a supreme fiction, instead of creating it, as the
Greeks did, for example, in the form of a mythology, we might choose
to create it in the image of a man: an agreed-on superman.
—Wallace Stevens, *Letters*

After the publication of *Harmonium* in 1923, Stevens faced
the problem, faced eventually by every serious artist, of how
he could continue to write poetry without repeating himself.
The poet, he decided, must come again to recognize the communal importance of his art. As much as Virgil's Rome, modern America needed a "central poetry": one answerable to
the contemporary desires of men for objects of belief, and
one in which the poet could credibly say "I" and mean "Man."
"It is / For that," Stevens wrote in *Notes*, "the poet is always
in the sun, / Patches the moon together in his room / To his
Virgilian cadences" (*CP* 407).

This new orientation toward a central poetry was announced in the poetry of *Ideas of Order*, Stevens' second volume, but Stevens evolved a myth of man as the hero of his
world very slowly, and only began to gain confidence in it a
full twenty years after the appearance of *Harmonium*. In the
chronicle of the hero in Stevens, 1942 stands out as Annus
Mirabilis. It was the year of *Parts of a World*, of "The Noble

Rider and the Sound of Words," and of *Notes toward a Supreme Fiction.* In *Parts of a World* Stevens is still preoccupied with destroying "romantic tenements of rose and ice" and is still feeling for the form of his myth. The single event which focused his thoughts with reference to the supreme fiction "created in the image of a man" seems to have been the invitation extended by his friend Henry Church to deliver at Princeton an address on the nature of poetry. The resulting essay, "The Noble Rider and the Sound of Words," speaks urgently of the loss of noble images of man in contemporary art; by the year's end Stevens' thinking had fulfilled itself in *Notes toward a Supreme Fiction.*

Stevens' creation of the heroic image, then, differs substantially in character from Whitman's. The appearance of Whitman's "Myself" seemingly out of thin air has always puzzled critics; as one of them puts it, "neither [Whitman's] heredity nor his temporary employment help much to explain how a relatively indolent odd-jobber and sometime journalist named Walter Whitman developed into Walt Whitman the poet."[1] The figure of the possible poet in Stevens, on the other hand, emerges slowly out of a background of failed or partial images. How to give a twentieth-century form to the persona Whitman called the Real Me is the most important concern of Stevens' poetry after 1942, but I shall be able to do it only partial justice. I hope mainly to establish the relevance of Whitman as a model and a symbol in Stevens' work. With this end in view I have divided my discussion into two parts. I shall begin with the poems of *Ideas of Order* where, stationed above a "cemetery of nobilities" (*NA* 35)—Stevens' metaphor for the poetry of the past—Stevens symbolizes the heroic idealism of poetic tradition in the figure of Walt Whit-

---

[1] R. W. B. Lewis, *Trials of the Word* (New Haven: Yale University Press, 1965), p. 5.

man, and announces the terms on which the poet in the sun may be reclaimed for earth. Then I shall discuss a number of poems from Stevens' late career which reveal his mythic hero as a secure symbol.

In 1935: The Hero on the Horizon

"Like Decorations in a Nigger Cemetery"

> In the far South the sun of autumn is passing
> Like Walt Whitman walking along a ruddy shore.
> He is singing and chanting the things that are part of him,
> The worlds that were and will be, death and day.
> Nothing is final, he chants. No man shall see the end.
> His beard is of fire and his staff is a leaping flame.   [CP 150]

"Like Decorations in a Nigger Cemetery" is one of the two or three long poems that give distinction to *Ideas of Order* (1935), others being "The Idea of Order at Key West" and, perhaps, "Academic Discourse at Havana." "The Idea of Order at Key West" has long been read and admired as an important document in Stevens' movement from *Harmonium* to the greatness of the late poems, but "Like Decorations in a Nigger Cemetery" has until very recently attracted no reader patient enough to penetrate its formal mysteries and describe its place in the development of Stevens' art. Now that Helen Vendler has performed this service[2] it is possible to see "Decorations" as perhaps even the central poem of *Ideas of Order*, focusing its themes and representing its uncertainties and pessimism more characteristically than does "The Idea of Order at Key West."

The subject of "Decorations" is whether poetry can be

[2] Vendler, *On Extended Wings* (Cambridge: Harvard University Press, 1969), pp. 65–74.

created out of doubt about the imagination. To some degree "Decorations" shares a theme with Coleridge's "Dejection," because its origin is a feeling of declining creativity, and the poem is an effort to express the fears that feeling inspires.

Formally, "Decorations" is composed of fifty numbered stanzas of different lengths which are, to borrow Vendler's expressive phrase, flagrantly discontinuous. In her opinion the discontinuity tends to make all the stanzas equally important, so that "Stevens' true subject in 'Decorations' becomes the complexity of mental response, the intimations, in all those fifty stanzas, of almost all possible responses to the decay that is its topic." Vendler believes Stevens chooses to express no preference among the attitudes the poem offers, "except by the implicit preference accorded by convention to the beginning and end."[3]

This preference, it seems to me, is fairly significant in "Decorations." Here as in any poem the reader's sense of meaning is guided by preferential attitudes both implicit and expressed within the context of the poem, and also by the poem's context within the volume *Ideas of Order*, which itself has an expressible theme. For one thing, the reader may distinguish stanzas having varying degrees of importance—two complementary kinds of stanzas. Some are, as Vendler observes, like haiku or Imagist poems, whose "meanings" reside in the spaces between the lines. These provide a sense of the weather of the poem, "things as they are" observed by a sensibility in an autumnal phase. Others are themselves distinctly evaluative, performing acts of judgment on the world of the poem. The stanzas collect thematically into patterns and take focus within

[3] Vendler, " 'Stevens' Like Decorations in a Nigger Cemetery,' " *Massachusetts Review*, VII (Winter 1966), 136–137. (This article, slightly revised, became Chapter III, "The Sausage Maker," in Vendler's *On Extended Wings*.)

each other's perspectives. References to motion and stillness, sun and frost, speech and silence, accumulate within range of one another, asking to be seen in design. The design, moreover, seems to be generated by the polarity established in the opening stanzas in the difference between a heroic poet of the past and the present narrator. The difference is explored and its meanings considered in the interior stanzas which are directed toward an end, are directed, in fact, toward the same end as many other poems in *Ideas of Order* and articulated in "The American Sublime":

> How does one stand
> To behold the sublime,
> To confront the mockers,
> The mickey mockers
> And plated pairs?
>
> . . . . .
>
> And the sublime comes down
> To the spirit itself,
>
> To the spirit and space,
> The empty spirit
> In vacant space.   [CP 130]

The interior stanzas of "Decorations" project answers to these questions, among which distinctions are made: some attitudes will do, others will not. The fatalist may be beguiled by autumn pears, the sensual fruits of summer's warmth (XXVIII), but the narrator refuses to be consoled for "*encore un instant de bonheur . . . / Are a woman's words unlikely to satisfy / The taste of even a country connoisseur*" (XLV). To the eye of the tired narrator (II) the world in November appears stagnant (XXXIV) or mechanical (XLI, XLVI); the ground is as blank as the sky (IV); nonetheless, "in between lies the sphere of my fortune" (IV); "invisible currents clearly circulate" (XXXIV); "music is not yet written but is to be" (XLVIII), for "the actual is a deft beneficence" (XXXI). Taking caution from Helen Vendler, however, one would not want to rest a case on this kind of sleight-of-hand arrangement of disparate lines. The argument for a sense of direction drawing the poem to a conclusion can best be supported by examining the first two and last four stanzas to see how they magnetize the details of the stanzas between, and also the themes of *Ideas of Order* itself.

The first stanza of "Decorations," quoted above, is the longest, and introduces the poem's most frequently recurring symbols. The most important of these symbols, for my purposes, is of course that of Walt Whitman, the poet in the sun. But it may be observed that the reference to Whitman is only one of four references to artists in the poem (the others are to Toulet, XV; Constable, XXVII; and Corot, XXXVIII), and that all these references furnish perspectives on the sentiment expressed in another poem of *Ideas of Order:* that though he is dead,

> We may return to Mozart.
> He was young and we, we are old.   [CP 132]

When the snow is falling and the streets are full of cries, such "lucid souvenir[s] of the past" become in "Mozart, 1935" the means "by which sorrow is released, / Dismissed, absolved, / In a starry placating." But "Decorations" is a more subtle poem: art, it says, offers not an escape but the example of achieved order. Hence the poet in the ruins of a new society reads Toulet "furtively, by candle and out of need"; yet such poems as Toulet's are said to be like "rouged fruits in early snow": unseasonal; for the narrator realizes—changing the metaphor—that he cannot transplant the serene landscapes of

Constable or Corot into the sphere of his own fortune with its stagnant waters, gray grass, mats of frost, and leafless trees. The stanza making use of Whitman is by far the most explicit in establishing the distance between the narrator and the imaginative power he craves.

This distance is suggested immediately in the opening lines: "In the far South the sun of autumn is passing / Like Walt Whitman . . ." (*CP* 150). It is autumn in the poem, but the sun—the "brave man" (*CP* 138) or "heroic power" (*CP* 375) —has already gone to another hemisphere. The wintry northern landscape is, of course, purely a landscape of the mind where the weather comes from the poet's thoughts and feelings; but he has chosen it in the poem that opens *Ideas of Order*, where "To be free again, to return to the violent mind / That is their mind, these men, and that will bind / Me round," he books passage on a ship headed north, "To the cold" (*CP* 118). However the image of the sun as Whitman is ambiguous. The feeling that he is absent is balanced against other implications. For one thing, Whitman is a native of Stevens' soil, and one of the basic tenets of this poem is Crispin's "Nota: his soil is man's intelligence / . . . That's [a principle] worth crossing seas to find" (*CP* 36). Moreover, the sun's power is, as always in Stevens, linked to poetry, the capacity to make music of the things that are part of one's world. And this is the sun of autumn, the heroic power of the season in which the narrator finds himself, the human season of death and loss, and the season in nature when reality is impoverished and brutal. Hence the song the heroic figure is singing, "Nothing is final . . . / No man shall see the end," offers truths as difficult of penetration as those offered by the Cumaean Sibyl, and just as important, but they have no power to warm the mind until the scope of their credibility can be found. Yet the poem does not reject them. It offers Whitman's words at its opening with the implication that they somehow might be made to fill the imagination's need.

At least, this is how I interpret the first stanza in terms of what immediately follows, where the narrator invokes a cycle positing the sun's return:

> Sigh for me, night-wind, in the noisy leaves of the oak.
> I am tired. Sleep for me, heaven over the hill.
> Shout for me, loudly and loudly, joyful sun, when you rise.
>   [*CP* 150]

All three of these natural symbols have important and consistent meanings in Stevens. The hill is generally a point of survey from which an order is discovered in reality, "The way, when we climb a mountain, / Vermont throws itself together" (*OP* 115). The autumnal wind, as Harold Bloom has noticed,[4] has in Stevens a specifically Shelleyan meaning as the destroyer who precedes the spring's renewal. It is associated with poetry in "Decorations" by being likened to a voice that says farewell (X), and by the poem's indication that the wind's act of destruction is paradoxically creative, since in tearing the leaves from the trees it exposes an underlying structure:

> It was when the trees were leafless first in November
> And their blackness became apparent, that one first
> Knew the eccentric to be the base of design.   [*CP* 151]

This leaflessness is conceived as a state necessary in the landscape of the mind as it is in nature. "Decorations" projects such leaflessness as an ideal condition of reality for certain purposes:

---

[4] Bloom, "The Central Man: Emerson, Whitman, Wallace Stevens," *Massachusetts Review*, VII (Winter 1966), 23ff.

> If thinking could be blown away
> Yet this remain the dwelling-place
> Of those with a sense for simple space.   [CP 153]

Taken together, then, the first two stanzas of "Decorations" establish the central concern of the poem as the loss—and the expectation of return—of something specific, a vital power of imagination that gives the world coherence and motion. There is no rhetorical formula of presentation as in Coleridge's "Dejection" or Wordsworth's "Intimations Ode," no "there was a time . . . but now . . ." Rather, the oppositions in "Decorations" are implied throughout the poem through juxtapositions of symbols and of attitudes. The sun is contemplated by a mind in a context of clouds and frost. The poet's stasis— his tiredness (II), his positioning as if at the center of a frozen field (IV)—is countered by the motion of the voices of creative sun and destroying wind, the ruddiness of Whitman's shore by the bare black and white of leafless trees and frost in a mental cemetery. Nor is there, except occasionally, so expressible a connection between the stanzas as occurs here at the beginning and again at the end. They are mostly fragmentary, disparate acts of a mind pressing back against the pressure of reality. Only the pressure of reality is constant in the poem, and "From this the poem springs" (CP 383), as Stevens says later in an equally pressured state. Yet the poem's diversity is limited. For an example of the way the symbolic motifs identified above reappear in new begettings, we may look at one of the more penetrable stanzas:

> From oriole to crow, note the decline
> In music. Crow is realist. But, then,
> Oriole, also, may be realist.   [CP 154]

The crow in his blackness seems most appropriate to the November landscape and possibly most like in voice to the speaker of "Decorations," but the oriole is both black and gold, the color of the sun. It may be, the poem suggests, that his euphonies partake as fully of reality as do the crow's croakings. Only at the end of the poem, however, from about XLVII on, does one begin to sense the direction in these observations, as the mind returns to the human figure in the landscape to say a few last words projecting possibilities for him.

What I am identifying as the ending movement of the poem is announced by a return at stanza XLVII to the image of the sun as a presence both in the narrator's mind and in the reality which the mind regards. In an interior stanza the weak autumnal sun had seemed to him "A tiger lamed by nothingness and frost" (CP 153). Now the narrator sees the sun as an abstraction again, what he will later call a "first idea" seeking a form:

> The sun is seeking something bright to shine on.
> The trees are wooden, the grass is yellow and thin.
> The ponds are not the surfaces it seeks.
> It must create its colors out of itself.   [CP 157–158]

At the beginning of "Decorations," when the sun had a poet's form, music issued from it. At the end, by the same logic, since the sun is only *feeling* for its form,

> Music is not yet written but is to be.
> The preparation is long and of long intent
> For the time when sound shall be subtler than we ourselves.
>   [CP 158]

The idea Stevens seems to be glimpsing here is expressed more directly in *Notes toward a Supreme Fiction:* the poetry that illuminates human nature always contains a hero who is "abler in the abstract than his singular, / More fecund as principle than particle" (CP 388). This is because he is an abstraction, an "unreal" more true than reality because it is an interpretation of reality, its meaning. A poem containing such a hero is capable of such affirmations as "nothing is final . . . / No man shall see the end." This is not such a poem. Still, Stevens implies, the modern analogues to Whitman's chant will have to be written in the context Stevens has chosen, under the disadvantages of the climate of "Decorations." The "drenching weather" of autumn reality, says the next stanza, has made him return to *people*, to find among them / Whatever it was he had found in their absence" (*CP* 158). His subject, in short, is to be man. This does not mean that Stevens has decided to become a "poet of the people" with all the connotations that phrase had in 1935. If this was ever in doubt, the last stanza makes it clear:

> Union of the weakest develops strength
> Not wisdom. Can all men, together, avenge
> One of the leaves that have fallen in autumn?
> But the wise man avenges by building his city in snow.

Building the city—civilized shelter, a place for men to live together—in snow has become the project of a man who has seen through the aesthetic alternatives, and has seen through them largely before our eyes in this or other poems of *Ideas of Order*. The fulfillment of that project he will come to call, in terms like those above, "a cure of the ground / Or a cure of ourselves that is equal to a cure / Of the ground" (*CP* 526). But at this point he is only aware of the disease, and not at all certain he will survive it.

From 1942 to 1955: Experience in Perihelion

> Here the sun,
> Sleepless, inhales his proper air, and rests.
> —"Credences of Summer"

The relevance of Walt Whitman to Wallace Stevens can be perceived most clearly in the poetry of Stevens from *Transport to Summer* through *The Rock*, for the last half of the *Collected Poems* contains most of Stevens' poems about the hero: the noble, affirmative, solitary, central man metaphorically identified with the sun. The context for this figure, and the source of his imaginative credibility, is the myth of imagination Stevens had evolved. The myth becomes the direct subject of such important late works as "Credences of Summer," "The Auroras of Autumn," and "The Rock." It involves the identification of creative imagination with both the sun and the earth, that is, with both the source and the ground of illumination, and emphasizes the importance of a productive opposition between the two. This formulation allowed Stevens to postulate for the imagination a winter solstice—a period when the mental sun illuminates but does not warm or generate life—and a summer solstice; a vernal state and an autumnal state. The late period of Stevens' poetry has much to say of particularly that latter state, the imagination's fall season. But here I want to discuss what Stevens once described as "High poetry":

> Experience in perihelion
>
> . . . . .
>
> The solemn sentences,
> Like interior intonations,
> The speech of truth in its true solitude,
> A nature that is created in what it says,
> The peace of the last intelligence.   [CP 490]

Stevens' late heroic poetry is of two types. In the first, as in Whitman's poetry of the Real Me, the hero speaks in the first person: "I celebrate myself." The poems of this type with which I shall be most concerned are *Notes toward a Supreme Fiction* and "The Bouquet."

The second type does not always use the hero as narrating persona, but rather is concerned with his image: what he looks like, and how his presence is felt. I will consider two of these images here: the image of the giant, Stevens' most consistent poetic representation of the modern poet, and the image of the ancestor or "bearded peer" (*CP* 494), of which the Whitman-sun of "Decorations" is an early type.

Notes toward a Supreme Fiction

This is Stevens' version of "Song of Myself." Its aesthetic form is not, as in Whitman, mythologized autobiography. Yet the face that Stevens finally places in the sun as the imagination's face—one slightly less godlike than the face of Phoebus Apollo—is the poet's own: at the end of *Notes* its hero is revealed to be "I." Both Whitman and Stevens aspired to the same achievement: to give the myth of Man a credible contemporary poetic form, and to provide thereby a ground for belief in the nobility and meaning of human experience which would "help people to live their lives" (*NA* 29). Whitman described this intention in his own work as "throw[ing] together for American use, a gigantic embryo or skeleton of Personality, fit for the West, for native models." Stevens' emphasis was on the skeleton rather than on the Personality; but the "I" of *Notes toward a Supreme Fiction* may nonetheless be viewed as the Real Me abstracted and reimagined.

If Stevens' purpose was like that of Whitman in "Song of Myself," he obviously viewed the project from a different perspective. Whitman—one of the American figures R. W. B. Lewis has called "American Adams"[5]—founds his fiction on the premise that man's condition is "different from what any-

---

[5] Lewis, *The American Adam*, pp. 28–53.

one supposed, and luckier" (*LG* 35). In "Song of Myself" imperfection is a kind of illusion with which the "Real" man has only tenuous and unexplored connections. It is visibly this aspect of the thought of Whitman and other Romantics that Stevens finds to be in need of revision. The proportional emphases of his own myth more closely resemble an account of Adam from Eden to Apocalypse. It begins in the assumption that man is redeemable but fallen. The theme of "Terra Paradise" (*CP* 263) is important in Stevens' work from the beginning, but his intention to write a kind of post-Christian analogue to the Biblical myth is suggested as early as "A Thought Revolved," one of the "Other Poems" that appeared with *The Man With the Blue Guitar* in 1937. In that poem Stevens differentiates between the poet's physical context—an "infernal world" composed of the banal: "cigar stores, / Ryan's lunch, hatters, insurance"—and the "metaphysical space" the poet inhabits.

> [There the poet's] hymns come crowding, hero-hymns,
>
> . . . . .
>
> Happy rather than holy but happy-high,
> Day hymns instead of constellated rhymes,
> Hymns of the struggle of the idea of god
> And the idea of man, the mystic garden and
> The middling beast, the garden of paradise
> And he that created the garden and peopled it.   [*CP* 185]

What this poem merely projects as possible, in *Notes* is fully worked out. In part one, "It Must Be Abstract," the poet locates the credibility of the idea of man as fallen but redeemable; in part two, "It Must Change," he gives validity to the idea of human salvation, in effect by redefining the terms "death" and "life"; in part three, "It Must Give Pleasure," he indicates how the breach between man and reality is closed by the act of imagination that cures the world in endlessly repeated apocalypse. From this description it can be seen, however, that if the Biblical myth is analogue, it is also a target of de-creation. Stevens aspires in *Notes* to give something like Whitman's immediacy and commonness to the representation of man as the "hero of his world" (*CP* 261) but to free it from the dogmatic, the merely personal, and the supernatural.

Stevens' unique instrument in achieving this purpose was the non-narrative form he devised for *Notes*. I have examined this form earlier with reference to "It Must Give Pleasure," but its character may usefully be restated here. Its basis is demonstration of the characteristic twofold activity of the imagination, described and labeled by Coleridge as primary and secondary. It will be recalled that Coleridge conceived of the imagination as having both an acutely perceptive stage, the primary, and an intensely active stage, the secondary, in which the mind either "dissolves, diffuses, dissipates, in order to recreate; or, where this is rendered impossible, . . . struggles to idealize and to unify" (*Biographia Literaria*, XIII). Stevens comes closest to devising a theoretical terminology for this twofold activity in his poem "The Glass of Water" (*Parts of a World*), where he sketches an analogy between the states "between two poles" (liquid and solid) of objects in physical reality, and the states of these objects in the imagination:

> That the glass would melt in heat,
> That the water would freeze in cold,
> Shows that this object is merely a state,
> One of many, between two poles. So,
> In the metaphysical, there are these poles.   [*CP* 197]

The two poles "in the metaphysical," or imagination, are the state of image and the state of idea. In one, the glass of water is seen as an enchanting image. The glass is being willfully transformed, and the rhythms tell us the mind is self-delighted with its activity:

> Here in the centre stands the glass. Light
> Is the lion that comes down to drink.
>
> . . . . .
>
>   the glass is a pool.
> Ruddy are his eyes and ruddy are his claws
> When light comes down to wet his frothy jaws
>
> And in the water winding weeds move round.   [*CP* 197]

In the other state, the glass of water is perception moving toward image: "the refractions, / The *metaphysica*, the plastic parts of poems" that "crash in the mind." The poem itself only hints at the theory it contains; its subject is the motion roused in the mind by acute perception, a motion from idea to image, and back. By the date of *Notes toward a Supreme Fiction*, the Coleridgean concept of imagination has become fundamental. Each of the three parts of *Notes* may be seen as divisible into halves, with the first five cantos imitating, generally, the movement of the secondary imagination toward the primary phase—dissolving, diffusing, dissipating, as Coleridge puts it—attempting to abstract "*metaphysica*" from existing forms in nature and in art. The last five cantos of each part of *Notes* represent the movement of the secondary imagination in its efforts to evolve symbolic forms adequate to those abstractions in resonance and clarity. As in Stevens' other meditative poems, the particular form of each canto is determined by the motion of the mind as it seeks first to know and then to represent its object. Fragmentariness, or at least the appearance of arbitrariness, thus becomes a convention of Stevens' meditative form, tokening the mind's restlessness and resourcefulness as it assaults its object, or sheds its insights in sustained inventive bursts of images.

With these observations made, we may turn again to the central poem of the hero as "I" in Stevens, *Notes toward a Supreme Fiction*. I have already described, in the preceding chapter, the manner in which the imagination's power to espouse reality is made, in the third part of *Notes,* proof of its authority. But the imaginative reasoning which makes possible the poet's recognition of himself as hero occupies the first part of the poem, "It Must Be Abstract."

This section of *Notes* has no conventional "argument," but rather what might be described as an expressible intention. It is a pedagogical demonstration—hence "notes"—of the manner in which the mind, thinking about Man, may move from a "fallen" state of ennui or frustration to a "redeemed" state of imaginative perception, "the vivid transparence / . . . [which] is peace" (*CP* 380). The first four cantos concern the aspects of human nature that must be accounted for in any credible formulation of the idea of man; the central canto discloses that to grasp the idea is only half the battle engaged by the aspirant, for to be poet he must also be able to give it utterance; the last five concern the creation of images, and offer critiques of various forms by which the abstract major man might be embodied, before at last choosing one of whom the poet may confidently say, "It is he." However, each of the cantos is a discrete poem, connected with the others not by a logic of rational progression, but through the influence of shared symbols and in desire for insight into the supreme subject.

Canto I begins *in medias res*, as if the reader were overhearing a dialogue already begun between a master poet and his apprentice. The master has suggested to his student, the "ephebe,"—if we may look for a moment at Stevens' words in another context—"the possibility of a supreme fiction, in which men could propose to themselves a fulfillment. In the creation of any such fiction, poetry would have a vital significance" (*LWS* 820). If the ephebe is to compose such fictions he must possess a clear sense of the term "supreme," and this is where he is instructed to begin:

> Begin, ephebe, by perceiving the idea
> Of this invention, this invented world,
> The inconceivable idea of the sun. [*CP* 380]

Of course, the ephebe already possesses "ideas of the sun" through his familiarity with poetry and myth, the traditional forms in which the idea of the "supreme" has been communicated to the generations. But Stevens has a particular idea of the sun in mind. Like Keats's youthful poet in *The Fall of Hyperion*, the possible poet of "It Must Be Abstract" is to be initiated into his vocation through confrontation of the myth that personifies creative power as the sun god Phoebus; and like Keats's poet the ephebe will by the end of the poem have been invested with that power. But in this part of *Notes* "the sun / Must bear no name" (*CP* 381); the ephebe's first act must be to remove the divine face from the sun in order to replace it, as his last act, with a human face. To "see [the sun] clearly in the idea of it" is to see it as the highest power, the transforming power of the mind. The *idea* of the sun has been confounded with its images and must be recaptured by the intellect of the present poet. The necessity of the ephebe to the supreme fiction lies here. Just as Phoebus, the archetypal poet, was both sun and son, so the ephebe who is to be Apollo's present form is a son or virile youth in the process of discovering the true nature of his creative power, of discovering *he* is the sun. "There was a project for the sun, and is."

In canto I, then, Stevens has slain the sun god Phoebus, rel-
egating him to the "cemetery of nobilities" (*NA* 35) which
contains the body of poetic tradition: "Let purple Phoebus
lie in umber harvest." He has added that "The death of one
god is the death of all." Yet the purpose of the poem is to
project a supreme fiction. Hence cantos II–IV become efforts
to arrive at an idea of Man superior to any idea of God which
has ever been evolved as the basis for a supreme fiction. The
problem with which these three cantos are, explicitly or im-
plicitly, concerned, is man's consciousness of living

> in a place
> That is not our own, and much more, not ourselves
> And hard it is in spite of blazoned days.   [*CP* 383]

Nature is a "myth" (*CP* 383) or invented world outside
man's comprehension: inhuman. Between the world and man
there is no common language, Stevens insists in canto IV; the
sea will never speak to him as it spoke to Whitman, for it
makes no voice, only "sounds" that are "pips / Of the sweep-
ing meanings that we add to them" (*CP* 384). Since desire
for meaning is such a common state for man, unanswered by
anything outside himself, man might easily regard himself as
fallen and unredeemed, but the poem will not allow it. The
fallenness described in IV is identical with redemption, the
poem argues; not cause but phase:

> not to have is the beginning of desire.
> To have what is not is its ancient cycle.   [*CP* 382]

The mind cannot station itself in a truth and the symbolic
forms that express it, however noble, without dimming into
"celestial ennui" (*CP* 381). Moreover, its activity is an "an-

cient cycle" moving from idea to image and back, with an effect like the sun's, creating not only seasonal weather but dawn after dawn:

> It is desire at the end of winter, when
>
> It observes the effortless weather turning blue
> And sees the myosotis on its bush.
> Being virile, it hears the calendar hymn.
>
> It knows that what it has is what is not
> And throws it away like a thing of another time,
> As morning throws off stale moonlight and shabby sleep.
> [CP 382]

The true correspondence between the sun and imagination as the highest power of each world, natural and human, is not the sun's immortality—an inhuman attribute embodied in the idea of Phoebus—but its cyclical movement from "winter," or the desire for clarity, to "summer," the satisfaction of that desire in imaginative form.

Finally, the proof of the imagination's essential innocence, as well as the mark of its redemption, is its power to save. In a passage which evokes Christian rhetoric and iconography with only partial irony, Stevens describes how the poem, agent of the imagination, both gives more abundant life and dissolves the breach man recognizes between himself and the world:

> The poem refreshes life so that we share,
> For a moment, the first idea . . . It satisfies
> Belief in an immaculate beginning
>
> And sends us, winged by an unconscious will,
> To an immaculate end. We move between these points:
> From that ever-early candor to its late plural

And the candor of them is the strong exhilaration
Of what we feel from what we think, of thought
Beating in the heart.   [*CP* 382]

In the discussion above I have been attempting to suggest the ways in which Stevens fulfills the title's claim that we are reading notes toward a "supreme" fiction. Making these critical generalizations has necessarily involved placing the poem within the perspective of the literary and mythical tradition it seeks to renew and continue. Thus I have drawn my analogies in terms of the traditional religious rhetoric which is one of Stevens' chief targets of de-creation, as he declares at canto IX:

The romantic intoning, the declaimed clairvoyance
Are parts of apotheosis, appropriate
And of its nature, the idiom thereof.

.   .   .   .   .
But apotheosis is not
The origin of major man.   [*CP* 387]

The only way to become a poet capable of supreme fictions, Stevens has told the ephebe, is to become first "an ignorant man again / And see the sun again with an ignorant eye" (*CP* 380). This means conscious avoidance of the old mythic "intonings." "The poet who writes the heroic poem that will satisfy all there is of us and all of us in time to come," Stevens wrote, "will accomplish it by the power of his reason, the force of his imagination, and in addition, the effortless and inescapable process of his own individuality" (*NA* 46). This is Stevens' own formulation at the end of canto IV, quoted above, for the process by which alien nature is received into the imagination and there transformed:

And still the grossest iridescence of ocean
Howls hoo and rises and howls hoo and falls.
Life's nonsense pierces us with strange relation.   [*CP* 383]

The first two lines of this stanza are the purest Stevens in language, sensibility, and tone; anyone else who spoke so in a poem would be recognized instantly as an imitator of Stevens. But it was a style developed, not received. The "difficulty of what it is to be" a poet capable of placing the mark of his own individuality on the poem is as much a theme of *Notes* as is the possibility of writing a supreme fiction. In "It Must Be Abstract" this theme develops directly out of the acknowledgment that we live in a world that is not ourselves, and becomes the subject of canto V, where the ephebe is reintroduced. Lion, elephant, and bear are by nature masters of the simple worlds they invent by being conscious; their poetry of roars, blares, and snarls expresses most satisfactorily their sense of themselves in reality.

> But you, ephebe, look from your attic window,
> Your mansard with a rented piano. You lie
>
> In silence upon your bed. You clutch the corner
> Of the pillow in your hand. You writhe and press
> A bitter utterance from your writhing, dumb,
>
> Yet voluble dumb violence. You look
> Across the roofs as sigil and as ward
> And in your centre mark them and are cowed.   [*CP* 384]

"The poem," Stevens says elsewhere, "is a struggle with the inaccessibility of the abstract" (*LWS* 434). How shall the poet give adequate voice to the life of man? The succeeding cantos of "It Must Be Abstract" do not answer this question directly, but as before offer demonstrations of the mind in the act of finding—this time of finding not the abstraction "man," which has been found in the preceding cantos, but of finding the verbal form in which he will be most credible as hero of a supreme fiction.

The last five cantos of "It Must Be Abstract" develop a line of thought somewhat more available to paraphrase. Canto VI states the proposition: the abstraction "man" must be realized in form, "blooded," or it can never be communicated. The statement is elliptical but the intention is clear: without poetic form the possible philosopher's man is "not to be loved or hated . . . [is] not to / Be spoken to, [is] without a roof, without / First fruits, without the virginal of birds" (*CP* 385). Therefore a mythic "falseness close to kin" is devised: not god but giant, man at once "visible" (because made in man's image) and "invisible" (because unreal, a fiction).

In the next canto the poet's mind moves back—with a tone of caution, but with pedagogical intent—from this image.

> It feels good as it is without the giant,
> A thinker of the first idea. Perhaps
> The truth depends on a walk around a lake.   [*CP* 386]

In his reference to the lake, and in the details of the lines that follow, Stevens seems to be considering the amount of truth that may be quarried from the Romantics' "declaimed clairvoyance." (As, for example, Coleridge in "Dejection": "O pure of heart! thou needest not ask of me / What this strong music in the soul may be!") Every life has "times of inherent excellence," to which this canto pays its respects in the last stanza. But Stevens' concern is not really whether great poetry can come from "balances that happen." Rather, he is concerned with whether a supreme fiction would have to have an active hero, one who struggled to be "thinker of the first idea" and labored hard to realize it in culturally significant forms. The lines describing "incalculable balances," the balances that come unwilled, contain their own critique. Such moments, Stevens implies, are not only slightly gross and mechanical in quality ("a kind of Swiss perfection comes / . . .

a familiar music of the machine / Sets up its Schwärmerei"),
they are also "extreme, fortuitous, personal": in short, not
central, or available to generalization.

With this settled, the poet takes up in canto VIII two other
questions. First, "can we *compose* a castle-fortress-home"
(italics mine), or adequate residence for the hero? And more
important, can we "set the MacCullough there as major
man?" By the MacCullough, Stevens told Hi Simons, he
meant "any man," the common man of whom the humanist
makes a hero. "The trouble with humanism" he wrote to
Simons, "is that man as God remains man, but there is an extension of man, the leaner being, in fiction, a possibly more
than human human, a composite human. The act of recognizing him is the act of this leaner being moving in on us" (*LWS*
434). In the course of canto VIII the "leaner being" moves
in on MacCullough, giving him a "greater aptitude and apprehension" and making of him the possible poet: it is as if
"the language suddenly with ease / Said things it had laboriously spoken." In response to the suggestion made in the preceding canto that we might get along as well without the idea
of the giant, this canto demonstrates his necessity to the supreme fiction. It revives Emerson's principle that "there is
One Man—present to all particular men only partially, or
through one faculty," but of whom, in our "right state" we
may all partake and whom we may all, in our "right state,"
nobly express.[6] "The MacCullough is MacCullough"; but he
has the capacity, being a man, to express "major man," the
human composite immanent in himself and everyone.

Having established, in canto VIII, the necessity of a single
noble hero for his myth, Stevens in cantos IX and X heralds
the rebirth of the image of man. We recall the opening of the
poem and its statement to the ephebe that the object of medi-

---

[6] Emerson, *Works*, I, 82–86.

tation in *Notes* is an "invented world" in which objective reality has already been converted into symbols. Stevens' method throughout the poem is, as he describes it elsewhere, first to seize the symbol "in savage scrutiny" (*CP* 376) until its outline dissolves and it is seen "clearly in the idea of it" (*CP* 380). After this, the idea is gradually allowed to assume new, ever more distinct and commonplace outlines. In canto I the object of recreative scrutiny was the sun as containing the divine face of Phoebus Apollo. In canto IX the unmistakable object of scrutiny and renewal is Christ, the Son of Man, the circumstances of his lowly birth making him an especially suggestive symbol for the purposes of the poem. All the images depicting the poet laboring at his desk are modulated to suggest the parallel. The newborn "major man," "Foundling of the infected past," comes "compact in invincible foils," evoking the gildings of mediaeval paintings; he comes at midnight, "Lighted . . . by the studious eye" as by a star; he is "swaddled," hymned, and cradled in repose "on a breast forever precious for that touch." Certain parts of Milton's "On the Morning of Christ's Nativity" seem to be implicated, as well as those Renaissance and Flemish paintings of the madonna in which such loving attention is devoted to the outstretched and benedictive hand of the infant. Yet these are implicated in order to be denied. Once the image has been born there is a tendency to fix it in a dogma. The poet works here specifically to avert that danger from his poem, and focuses the end of the canto in eloquent affirmation of the credibility of this nativity: that being the continual regeneration, out of the union of studious eye and yearning heart, of the heroic idea of man:

> He is and may be but oh! he is, he is,
> This foundling of the infected past, so bright,
> So moving in the manner of his hand.

Yet look not at his colored eyes. Give him
No names. Dismiss him from your images.
The hot of him is purest in the heart.   [CP 388]

Canto X follows, in its first half, with a summary of the abstract content of "It Must Be Abstract," which may be paraphrased thus:

1. The most important idea with which the poet may concern himself is the idea of man.
2. The poem about man must contain a hero who is
   a. like the sun, a "Happy fecundity, flor-abundant force," and
   b. not an exception, like Phoebus or Christ, but rather "the heroic part of the commonal."

But canto X has a dramatic structure, and the pedagogical summary with which it opens is used to remind us that the poem began as a dialogue. The narrator's lecture is suddenly interrupted by a question from the ephebe:

The major abstraction is the commonal,
The inanimate, difficult visage. Who is it?

What rabbi, grown furious with human wish,
What chieftain, walking by himself, crying
Most miserable, most victorious,

Does not see these separate figures one by one,
And yet see only one, in his old coat,
His slouching pantaloons, beyond the town,

Looking for what was, where it used to be?
Cloudless the morning. It is he.   [CP 388–389]

Rabbi and chieftain are here symbols of heroic but temporarily powerless types, for the myths that gave authority to their actions no longer consolidate an entire culture. Their function is to testify to the need for an inclusive myth which will reunite what Emerson called "the One Man," now dispersed into social functions. The cloudless morning tokens that the way has been cleared for the sun-gazing the ephebe will have to do in order to restore a visage, this time a human one, to the myth that tells man of himself:

> It is of him, ephebe, to make, to confect
> The final elegance, not to console
> Nor sanctify, but plainly to propound.   [CP 389]

At the beginning of this discussion I claimed that one problem Stevens solves in *Notes* is how to make the poet the hero of his own poem. The way for this identification of himself as present embodiment of major man has been prepared by the structure of the argument in "It Must Be Abstract," which concludes that to be credible the supreme fiction must take as its subject the heroic part of the commonal. This structure —the insistent identification of high with low—is repeated in "It Must Give Pleasure," where in canto VII the narrator dismisses the Canon Aspirin's "complicate . . . amassing harmony" because of its derivation from outworn fictions, both of church and state, which even though institutionalized do not partake of the commonal, are "imposed" rather than "discovered." In an effort to correct the Canon's "angelic" vision, the narrator projects the image of an angel that more satisfies human desire—one who, leaping out of heaven, "forgets the golden centre, the golden destiny" and "grows warm in the motionless motion of his flight" (*CP* 404). The full significance of this gesture is not immediately obvious, but will be understood by the reader who remembers how frequently Stevens uses "motion" as metaphor for the "living" quality in art, the mind's perceptive assent to imaginative form. Thus, the "One of Fictive Music" is described as she who gives "motion to perfection" (*CP* 87), and the ur-poet of "The

Auroras of Autumn," himself motionless, is said to be "of motion the ever-brightening origin" (*CP* 414). The questions that follow on the narrator's act of imagination indicate his recognition that heroic art arises out of the heights, and depths, of *everyman's* experience. "There is a month, there is a year, there is a time / In which majesty is the mirror of the self" (*CP* 405). The angel in the "lapis-haunted air" of the narrator's imagination is one expression of the "expressible bliss" that comes at times to every man who has thought enough; angels, "if only imagined but imagined well" (*CP* 385), are therefore real, and are also part of the commonal.

This is the realization "that pulls tight the final ring" (*CP* 442), as Stevens puts it in another poem. The narrator has discovered himself, being merely a man, to be both the potential author and the potential subject of a supreme fiction complete with angels: both he who can set in motion "The luminous melody of proper sound" (*CP* 404), and he of whom the "final elegance" can be confected. This is the discovery celebrated in the next canto:

> I can
> Do all that angels can. I enjoy like them,
> Like men besides, like men in light secluded,
>
> Enjoying angels.   [*CP* 405]

In other words, the poet writes of angels—and of Phoebus—by writing of man, and he writes of man by writing of his own expressible bliss, and whatever else fills his life and thought. The supreme fiction, says the end of *Notes,* is a song of myself.

"The Bouquet"

As I suggested above, there are many poems in the last three volumes of Stevens' *Collected Poems* in which the narrator represents himself as at the perihelion of vision, as a man "in light secluded, / Enjoying angels." These poems explore a variety of subjects, but are identifiable as a group by the tone of confidence, serenity, and simplicity with which they affirm the energies of imagination. It must be emphasized that they are not to be thought the "typical voice" of the late poems, as the voice of the Real Me may be called typical in the early Whitman. Far more characteristic is the nostalgic and death-shadowed joy of the voice at the end of "The Auroras of Autumn" who meditates "in winter's nick" (*CP* 421); this is the note sounded especially in the final volume of the collection and sustained so beautifully in Stevens' last great poem, "The Rock." I will deal in their turn with the place of these poems in Stevens' mythology of imagination. But first it is important to see that Stevens, like Whitman, had a fully developed myth treating of the virility of the imagination, its capacity to give life and to keep life in existence. To the poet in perihelion the question of death is either irrelevant or is raised in order to be denied, for his position at an apex of consciousness allows him a perspective from which immortality is a credible idea. This is the theme of several poems by Stevens, but we may single out "The Bouquet" for attention because of its resemblance to Whitman's "Crossing Brooklyn Ferry."

"The Bouquet" is concerned to some degree with the question of what the poet adds of himself to his poem. It begins with the observation that objects—in this case a shaggy bunch of flowers—are occasionally observed in such a way as to become things "in an inner world, / Suspended in temporary jauntiness" (*CP* 448): temporary because they are apprehended in the metaphors or awarenesses of resemblance they stir in the mind, "apparitions suddenly gone / And no less suddenly here again" (*CP* 448). The next three sections explore the meaning and content of those instants of enhanced vision. Then, with the calculated nonchalance of Whitman tossing his own "bunch poem" by the wayside,[7] Stevens in the last section overturns the bouquet, lets it slop over the edge of the table, and leaves it lying on the floor (*CP* 453).

It is not this cavalier ending, however, but the meditative central sections of the poem, particularly section II, which provoke comparison with "Crossing Brooklyn Ferry." Stevens argues that the bouquet viewed imaginatively is seen with an "other eye," one whose vision conducts us to a welcoming, commonal reality:

> One enters, entering home,
> The place of meta-men and para-things,
>
> And yet still men though meta-men, still things
> Though para-things.   [*CP* 449]

These lines are the metaphoric version of Stevens' statement in "Effects of Analogy" that "to determine the relation of the poet to his subject . . . would be simple if he wrote about his own world. We could compare it with ours. But what he writes about is his sense of our world" (*NA* 119). One of Stevens' illustrations of this effect in art is a brief and late poem by Whitman. The allusion to Whitman, though trivial in itself, gains interest when, knowing that "The Bouquet" and the essay were composed within a few months of each other,[8] we observe the details of Stevens' portrait of the meta-men for their striking resemblance to the narrator who comes

---

[7] See Whitman in "Spontaneous Me" (originally titled "Bunch Poem"): "this bunch pluck'd at random from myself, / It has done its work—I toss it carelessly to fall where it may" (*LG* 105).

[8] "Effects of Analogy" was composed in February–March 1948 (see *LWS* 579) to be read as a Bergen lecture at Yale, March 18, 1948. "The Bouquet" was one of a group of poems submitted for publication in early August 1948 (see *LWS* 609), a group on which Stevens seems to have been working at least as early as May of that year: see

"face to face" with the "bright flow" of reality in "Crossing Brooklyn Ferry" and feels its "glories strung like beads on my smallest sights and hearings." The meta-men in Stevens' poem are those

> For whom no blue in the sky prevents them, as
> They understand, and take on potency,
> By growing clear, transparent magistrates,
>
> Bearded with chains of blue-green glitterings
> And wearing hats of angular flick and fleck,
> Cold with an under impotency that they know.
>
> . . . . .
>
> Through the door one sees on the lake that the white duck
>   swims
> Away—and tells and tells the water tells
> Of the image spreading behind it in idea.
>
> The meta-men behold the idea as part
> Of the image, behold it with exactness through beads
> And dewy bearings of their light-locked beards.   [CP 449]

Stevens' poem almost seems to be a reading of "Crossing Brooklyn Ferry." It is as if the world mediated by Whitman's sensibility—complete even to the "dark patches" thrown on Whitman's poem at lines 65 ff (section 6, *LG* 162–163)—has been received whole into Stevens' mind and is refracted back to us, interpreted, in these lines. It would probably not be possible to determine the amount of direct influence present, that is, to determine whether in the course of preparing his essay "Effects of Analogy" Stevens paused over "Crossing Brooklyn Ferry" as well as "A Clear Midnight," the poem by

---

LWS 596 for Stevens' jottings toward what became "Our Stars Come from Ireland," one of the group submitted with "The Bouquet."

Whitman which he quotes. Yet I think the reader is meant to sense, if not to recognize, an allusion here, just as further on[9] he seems meant to recall certain impressionist still-life paintings. I venture this speculation because "The Bouquet," in sections III and IV, claims that the artist, in adding *himself* to reality—giving us "his sense of our world"—adds an absolute value. When we read a poem we discover a human meaning in reality, an effect Stevens calls a "doubling"—"the real made more acute by an unreal" (*CP* 451).

This claim has, of course, been made before by Stevens; "To the One of Fictive Music" uses nearly the same words. But it is made a little more largely in "The Bouquet," where Stevens also ascribes a *timeless* quality to an object imagined well. The aesthetic image, he says, stands as "sign / Of today, of this morning, of this afternoon" (*CP* 451). In short, he builds into "The Bouquet" the elements of Whitman's credo in "Crossing Brooklyn Ferry," that in the poem both the poet and the objects he treats have been given form which transcends mortality, and that they may be contacted again in the poem, with almost shocking immediacy. "Closer yet I approach you" (*LG* 163), Whitman says of himself across a hundred years, and of the river:

> You furnish your parts toward eternity,
> Great or small, you furnish your parts toward the soul.
>
> [*LG* 165]

And Stevens acquiesces to this, at least in principle:

> The bouquet,
> Regarded by the meta-men, is quirked
>
> And queered by lavishings of their will to see.
>
> . . . . .

[9] See lines 37–50 of "The Bouquet" (*CP* 450).

It is a symbol, a sovereign of symbols
In its interpretations voluble,

Embellished by the quicknesses of sight,

. . . . .

The infinite of the actual perceived,
A freedom revealed, a realization touched,
The real made more acute by an unreal.   [CP 451]

We must linger a moment over the observation that Stevens does not extend the consideration of immortality to himself in this poem, because all the difference between the two poets may be seen to lie in the difference between "I" and "meta-men" as names for the speakers of the poems. The Real Me is Whitman's personification for his imagination, and we have seen how respectfully Whitman regarded him. But writing poems was only one of the things the man did in a day. It is one of the pleasures of reading Whitman to hear him invoke that self who is not in the mood for making poems; in fact, he is the voice who after 1860 consistently was allowed the last word in *Leaves of Grass:*

From behind the screen where I hid I advance personally solely to you.

Camerado, this is no book,
Who touches this touches a man.   [LG 505]

Stevens, on the other hand, seemed to believe that this personal a voice was a drastic intrusion in a poem. His ideas on the subject are stated succinctly in "The Creations of Sound":

If the poetry of X was music,

. . . . .

. . . we should not know

. . . . .

That X is an obstruction, a man
Too exactly himself, and that there are words
Better without an author, without a poet,

Or having a separate author, a different poet,
An accretion from ourselves, intelligent
Beyond intelligence, an artificial man

At a distance, a secondary expositor,
A being of sound, whom one does not approach
Through any exaggeration. From him, we collect.   [CP 311]

When at the end of "Crossing Brooklyn Ferry" Whitman cries to the river "You furnish your parts to the soul," he does not only have in mind that concept of soul described by Emerson in "Self-Reliance" as the force of intellect which does not "see the face of men . . . [nor] hear any name . . . [but] raised over passion beholds identity."[10] Whitman has in mind his own individual being, as well:

Who knows but I am enjoying this?
Who knows, for all the distance, I am as good as looking at
you now, for all you cannot see me?   [LG 163]

But in Stevens' completed mythology of imagination, "I" is never more nor less than the metaphorical identity of "major man," the heroic, "commonal" sensibility with whom the narrator identifies himself at the end of *Notes*. His anonymity, in fact, accords with the ideal Stevens proposes in "The Figure of the Youth as Virile Poet," representing himself as "no more than a process," the voice of an imagination "standing in the radiant and productive atmosphere" of his own sense of the world "and examining first one detail of that world, one particular, and then another, as he finds them by chance, and observing many things that seem to be poetry without any

---

[10] Emerson, *Works*, II, 68–69.

intervention on his part, as, for example, the blue sky" (*NA* 59)—or the bouquet. And yet for all Stevens' principled and careful elimination of the merely personal from his work, I think no one would argue that his poetry lacks the quality of having emerged from "the effortless and inescapable processes of his own individuality" (*NA* 46), a quality Stevens deems essential to heroic poetry. Rather, in Stevens the personality informs the poem, can be distinguished in it but not separated from it. This effect is described toward the end of "The Bouquet." Perhaps, the poet muses, the colors of the symbol "assume / In the eye a special hue of origin" (*CP* 451); but if they do, this hue is "crystal crystal-white"—in other words, a transparence, a color like the sun's that is almost invisible—

And yet is there, a presence in the way.   [*CP* 452]

Two Symbols: Giant and Ancestor

Having examined at length the fulfillment, in the heroic "I" or narrating consciousness, of Stevens' desire to achieve a *voice* for the possible poet, we may now turn briefly to the fulfillment of his efforts to achieve for the hero an externalized symbolic *form*. I have pointed out that in the poetry through *Parts of a World* Stevens could not decide, as he puts it in "Examination of the Hero in a Time of War," whether to "Make him of mud, for every day," or, "In a civiler manner," to

> make him of winter's
> Iciest core, a north star, central
> In our oblivion, of summer's
> Imagination, the golden rescue.   [*CP* 275]

In *Notes toward a Supreme Fiction* we have seen Stevens decide on a "pensive giant prone in violet space" (*CP* 387), and from that date on, "it is a giant, always, that is evolved" (*CP*

442). Between "Examination" and *Notes* occurred a remarkable period of creativity whose effect on Stevens' work was something like that described in a later poem as "the way, when we climb a mountain, / Vermont throws itself together" (*OP* 115). "Chocorua to Its Neighbor," one of the poems from the early period of *Transport to Summer*, seems to have been "the one about the credible hero" (*OP* 117) written from the mountain as "Examination" was written from the plain. For after "Chocorua to Its Neighbor" the giant is a sure image, and one that becomes a direct object of meditation in "Primitive Like an Orb."

The giant is a symbol that seems to have satisfied Stevens as providing an identity for the concept of "essential imagination," making it a credible "object of belief" (*LWS* 370). The giant is an image of man enlarged beyond association with any individual biography or with any specific social role. He is close in conception to Emerson's Man Thinking—but embellished, to serve the imagination's need for delightful forms at the same time it serves the reason's need for truth to reality (*NA* 42). It is perhaps Stevens' most original contribution to the myth of man that his giant is so transcendently a figure of brilliance and joy:

> in bright excellence adorned, crested
> With every prodigal, familiar fire,
> And unfamiliar escapades: whirroos
> And scintillant sizzlings such as children like.   [*CP* 442]

This emphasis on the youth and dazzle of the giant may be best understood if we perceive his place in the mythology of imagination completed in the volume *Transport to Summer*. The giant is the human embodiment of the ultimate, which "must be good and is," described in "Credences of Summer," "the youth, the vital son" (*CP* 375) equated in the poem with the midsummer sun arrested at the zenith and fixed in eternal foliage to stand as brilliant emblem of the mind's power (*CP* 373). "Stripped of remembrance," Stevens says, "it displays its strength," and in its vivid repose it becomes a "rock" sustaining us in certainty of human adequacy (*CP* 375). These, as we have seen, are abstractly the qualities of the consciousness of the heroic "I," narrator of *Notes toward a Supreme Fiction*, "The Bouquet," and other late poems. Objectified, they culminate in the symbol of the giant.

But this heroic power has also another face in Stevens, a bearded or ancient face discovered in the autumnal phase of imagination as the face of the youthful giant was discovered in the summer phase. In Stevens' mythology, autumn is consistently represented as the time of the imagination's need, a post-creative period when in order to enter a new creative cycle the mind begins a process of detachment from its own creations—"form gulping after formlessness" (*CP* 411). This movement will eventually carry it to winter's icy and motionless clarity of perception. But in the autumnal phase the mind is nostalgic, or, more precisely, reflective about its origins, and is typically represented as searching for "forms of thought" (*CP* 432) which have enduring vitality. We have observed this process in *Ideas of Order* in a mode chiefly de-creative, with the poet's mind attacking false images and forms, and withholding belief. *The Auroras of Autumn* as a volume is replete with the alternative mode: the mind discovering and acknowledging the livingness of the past and the enduring capacity of things imagined well to elicit belief. The representative man—almost the only man—of *The Auroras of Autumn* is the "scholar," who appears variously as rabbi, savant, lecturer, "mistress of an idea," rhetorician, student, or simply Man Reading. The typical "action" in the poetry of *The Auroras of Autumn* brings this scholarly figure—sometimes

merely the consciousness of the narrator in an autumnal state
of need for enlightment—into contact with some form out of
the "huge imaginations" of poetic tradition, as Stevens calls
them in "The Noble Rider" (*NA* 23). This is the action represented, for example, in "Study of Images I," in terms of an
"awakening" within images, a quickening of imaginative life
"within the very object that we seek, / Participants of its being" (*CP* 463). It is what happens to the ghosts who come
back to hear the large red man read from the poem of life
(*CP* 423), and what happens to José after reading the novel,
when he discovers its characters within himself, "hidden and
alive," and "trembles to be so understood" (*CP* 458–459).
This regenerative process might be described generally as union with an image of "father," and results in a sense of completion, of resting within a knowledge that satisfies desire. It
will be recalled that this is what Whitman looked for in "As
I Ebb'd with the Ocean of Life" when he threw himself on
Paumanok's strand as on the breast of a father, and pleaded

> Touch me with your lips as I touch those I love,
> Breathe to me while I hold you close the secret of the mur-
>   muring I envy.   [*LG* 255]

In Stevens, however, the father so sought is not nature—even
in the guise of a sanctified place—but tradition, and union with
the image in Stevens is never described in sexual metaphors.
It is captured perhaps most poignantly in the image of Aeneas
bearing Anchises on his back out of burning Troy, for love
and honor's sake. This is the configuration used in "The Figure of the Youth as Virile Poet" (*NA* 52–53) and in "Recita-
tion after Dinner" to convey the idea of the "survival of a
good that we have loved" (*OP* 88): the preservation of ancient human truths in a new intelligence, so that, in the poem's
terms,

The father keeps on living in the son, the world
Of the father keeps on living in the world
Of the son.   [*OP* 87]

But the Anchises-like father—who is a burden on the young
intelligence as well as its progenitor (*NA* 53)—is only one of
the forms the image takes in Stevens. It is vitally associated as
well with a heroic and native poetry: in "The Auroras of
Autumn" it appears as the inexhaustible conjuror of aesthetic
form (sections IV–V). In "An Ordinary Evening in New
Haven," XIX, this concept of the image culminates in a
prophecy which, very much in the spirit of Whitman's 1855
Preface to *Leaves of Grass*, projects the advent of a poet-
priest for "this present colony of a colony / Of colonies"; and
the identity Stevens offers for him is highly reminiscent of the
Whitman-sun with which we began:

> A figure like Ecclesiast,
> Rugged and luminous, chants in the dark
> A text that is an answer, although obscure.   [*CP* 479]

Thus, in his late poetry, Stevens found a way to bring the
heroic power which was associated in *Ideas of Order* with
Whitman into a productive relation with his own creative
consciousness. Comparison of the narrators of the two volumes in which this feat is accomplished, *Transport to Summer*
and *The Auroras of Autumn*, makes possible a few generalizations about the progress of Stevens' career as poet between
1936 and 1950. The narrator of *Ideas of Order* looks with
ennui, contempt, or something resembling despair at the ambitious ideas of order left behind by other imaginations and
is explicitly critical of his own completed *oeuvre* in this regard ("Farewell to Florida," "Sailing After Lunch," "A Fad-
ing of the Sun"). Though he bravely predicts a freshening of
imagination and emergence from creative lassitude, he sug-

gests that the problem goes deep and locates it in the quality of his thought: his mind is "muddy" (*CP* 147), "smaller than the eye" (*CP* 161). His situation, then, is the opposite of that Coleridge describes in "Dejection"; he seems not to have thought *enough* ("Sad Strains of a Gay Waltz," "Lions in Sweden," "Mozart," "Winter Bells," "Academic Discourse at Havana," "The Reader," "Mud Master," "A Fish Scale Sunrise," "Delightful Evening"). This spirit enters even into "The Idea of Order at Key West," the volume's major poem, for it is the lady, not the narrator, who makes transcendent song; the poem ends with the question of *how* poetry accomplishes the transformation of reality. The poetry collected into *Transport to Summer*, however, gives new vitality to the tradition of affirmation from which the narrator of "Decorations" places himself at such a distance. *Notes toward a Supreme Fiction* furnishes a kind of manual for the writing of such poetry, demonstrating how *de*-creation—the brilliant mode of *Parts of a World*—becomes a positive phase in the creative process. In *Transport to Summer* Stevens may be seen to have removed himself from the cemetery of "Decorations" to the heights of "the natural tower of all the world" (*CP* 373). In the subtle manner of certain Renaissance painters, he has left us his portrait:

> It is the old man standing on the tower,
> Who reads no book. His ruddy ancientness
> Absorbs the ruddy summer and is appeased,
> By an understanding that fulfills his age,
> By a feeling capable of nothing more. [*CP* 374]

When autumn with its naked-making wind (*CP* 415, 437) again comes to Stevens' *Collected Poems*, it touches a mind better prepared to deal with it. Typical of the narrator of *The Auroras of Autumn* is a mood of serenity rather than frustration and self-doubt. The typical action of *The Auroras of Autumn,* as I have suggested, places the poet in fruitful relation with his own past and with the tradition he has sought to revitalize. An eye alert for mastered repetitions in Stevens' poetry can even discover in *Auroras* a revision of the configuration of narrator and heroic power recorded in "Like Decorations in a Nigger Cemetery." This occurs in "Things of August," which begins by echoing the affirmations attributed to Whitman in the earlier poem:

> Nothing is lost, loud locusts. No note fails.
> These sounds are long in the living of the ear.   [CP 489]

The words attributed to Whitman—"Nothing is final . . . / No man shall see the end" (*CP* 150)—become true for Stevens by the time of "Things of August," "because we wanted it so" (*CP* 495). Though so inappropriate as to seem ironic in the context of "Decorations," they are offered in "Things of August" as

> A text of intelligent men
> At the centre of the unintelligible,
> As in a hermitage, for us to think,
> Writing and reading the rigid inscription.   [CP 495]

What lies between the first and second autumns recorded in Stevens' *Collected Poems* is the consolidation of a myth of imagination which embodies all the ramifications of the idea "It Must Change." The autumnal sensibility of *Ideas of Order* seems beset by fear that its vital power has been exhausted; but the poems in that volume, particularly "Like Decorations in a Nigger Cemetery," identifying the poetic imagination with the sun, hold rudiments of the myth that explains the regeneration of creative power. We may trace the evolution of that myth by examining the significance of a single metaphor: the metaphor that identifies poetry with leaves of grass that "cure" the ground of the real.

Chapter 5

Whitman and Stevens: Nature in the Form of a Man

Up just as much out of fathomless workings fermented and thrown,
A limp blossom or two, just as much over waves floating, drifted at
    random,
Just as much for us that sobbing dirge of Nature,
Just as much whence we come that blare of the cloud-trumpets,
We, capricious, brought hither we know not whence, spread out before
    you,
You up there walking or sitting,
Whoever you are, we too lie in drifts at your feet.
                                    —"As I Ebb'd with the Ocean of Life"

A season changes color to no end,

Except the lavishing of itself in change,
As light changes yellow into gold and gold
To its opal elements and fire's delight.
                . . . . .
This is nothing until in a single man contained,
Nothing until this named thing nameless is,
And is destroyed.   —"The Auroras of Autumn"

In my discussion of Whitman and Stevens so far I have
been suggesting the relevance to Stevens of Whitman as an
achieved myth-maker and as the American continuator of
the Romantic tradition. Now I wish to examine the differences in the myths Stevens and Whitman evolved.

The fictive hero each poet conceives is an abstraction from
the self. He transcends the personality of the man; he expresses the poet's visionary perception of the divinity of Man.

He has an enemy, however—the poet's power of self-criticism. Once the heroic ego has been extrapolated from life and fixed as a symbol in a symbolic context, he is vulnerable to the poet's innate iconoclasm. As Wallace Stevens puts it:

> Say that even this complete simplicity
> Stripped one of all one's torments, concealed
> The evilly compounded, vital I
> And made it fresh in a world of white,
>
>   . . . . .
>
> There would still remain the never-resting mind,
> So that one would want to escape, come back
> To what had been so long composed.
> The imperfect is our paradise.   [CP 193–194]

Hence, in the myth of each poet there is a twofold movement, up and down: one which abstracts and idealizes the heroic self, and one which disintegrates the formulated ideal.

In Whitman this archetype of growth and decay is visible within the poetic autobiography which can be deduced from Whitman's text by arranging the poems—as Whitman did not choose to do—according to the stages of maturation they describe. The myth of the hero has a prehistory in the child's earliest questionings of reality ("There Was a Child Went Forth"), but its action proper is initiated by the boy's discovery of the poetic self latent in the common self ("Out of the Cradle Endlessly Rocking"): the potential Real Me. There follows for the possible poet a period of disguised or secret preparation during which he wanders unknown among his fellows, "absorbing and gathering" ("Starting from Paumanok," "The Sleepers"). Then, having reached maturity, he sets his chants in motion; he becomes "the friendly and flowing savage" compelling by his very form a spiritual regeneration among his countrymen ("Song of Myself," "Song of the Open Road," "Crossing Brooklyn Ferry," "Spontaneous Me"). Intuiting that an actual man is only a temporary and vulnerable incarnation of the Real Me ("As I Ebb'd with the Ocean of Life"), he bids his readers farewell "while my pleasure is still at the full" ("So Long!"). In Whitman's mythic plot the Real Me emerges from primal matter and then dies back into it, awaiting rebirth:

> Dear friend whoever you are take this kiss,
> I give it especially to you, do not forget me,
> I feel like one who has done work for the day to retire awhile,
> I receive now again of my many translations, from my avataras ascending, while others doubtless await me,
> An unknown sphere more real than I dream'd, more direct, darts awakening rays about me, *So long!*
> Remember my words, I may again return,
> I love you, I depart from materials,
> I am as one disembodied, triumphant, dead.   [*LG* 506]

In Stevens' myth, the analogous form is not the human cycle from birth to death, but the cycle of seasons from winter to winter. Rather than on physical growth and decline, Stevens' central metaphors are based on foliation and purgation. Stevens' mythic plot may be described in Emerson's words as "an apprenticeship to the truth that around every circle another can be drawn; that there is no end in nature, but every end is a beginning" ("Circles"). The imagination is salvaged, in the mental year, by divesting itself of its own foliage, growths of ideas in the mind. The elements of this symbolic system appear to have their experiential base in Stevens' extraordinary attentiveness to weather. Stevens often mentioned the influence of the climate on his state of mind—as in the letter he wrote to Barbara Church in October 1951:

I have been saying to myself pretty constantly of late that life is a dull life. That may have been the result of the long spell of dry weather: very good for chrysanthemums, which seem to prosper on aridity and monotony, but not at all good for a man living in a very small spot and disliking aridity and monotony when, by being continued, they become reality itself. Perhaps poetry, instead of being the rather meaningless transmutation of reality, is a combat with it; and perhaps the thing to do . . . is to pick a fight with it. In any case, yesterday and today, when the weather has been constantly changing . . . and when the air has been all colors with the leaves which are turning and falling and covering everything, the stale reality of this last summer seems to have come, or to be coming, to an end. [*LWS* 621]

However, the end of each cycle is the beginning of another. The autumnal mind becomes a seedbed, so that in a poem concerning autumn one often finds Stevens reading or listening to a book written by someone else.

> Over all these the mighty imagination triumphs
> Like a trumpet and says, in this season of memory,
> When the leaves fall like things mournful of the past,
>
> . . . . .
>
> Be still. The *summarium in excelsis* begins . . .
> Flame, sound, fury composed . . . Hear what he says,
> The dauntless master, as he starts the human tale.
>
> [*CP* 456]

The difference in the myths of these two poets, then, can best be located by comparing their handlings of the end of a cycle of imagination, the period of crisis which follows upon a period of creativity. As I observed earlier, W. H. Auden has lucidly described the quality of this post-creative stage: "In the eyes of others a man is a poet if he has written one good poem. In his own he is only a poet at the moment when he is making his last revision to a new poem. The moment before, he was still only a potential poet; the moment after, he is a man who has ceased to write poetry, perhaps forever."[1] In the myths of both Stevens and Whitman that moment is metaphorically associated with autumn and involves an identification between the cycle of nature and the poet's own creative imagination, an identification which issues in the symbol of his poems as leaves. But leaves of grass stand for different things in Whitman and Stevens. Because the form of Whitman's myth identifies the natural year with a single human life, autumn becomes the season of death, and fallen leaves a symbol for the ineffectuality of the works of man:

> As I wend to the shores I know not,
> As I list to the dirge, the voices of men and women wreck'd,
> As I inhale the impalpable breezes that set in upon me,
> As the ocean so mysterious rolls toward me closer and closer,
> I too but signify at the utmost a little wash'd-up drift,
> A few sands and dead leaves to gather,
> Gather, and merge myself as part of the sands and drifts.
>
> [*LG* 254]

Since the myth of the Real Me has a biographical form, Whitman had to postulate mortality as its conclusion—if only to demonstrate that the Real Me is indifferent to the thought of his own death:

> And as to you Life I reckon you are the leavings of many
>   deaths,
> (No doubt I have died myself ten thousand times before.)
>
> [*LG* 87]

An attitude of indifference is fundamental to the ideology of Whitman's prophetic vision, which has little to do with death. "Stop this day and night with me and you shall possess the origin of all poems," he wrote in 1855, a line which, unaltered, is retained through all editions of *Leaves of Grass*, and

---

[1] Auden, *The Dyer's Hand*, p. 41.

might well be the book's epigraph. The poetry of Whitman's later age is largely diffuse and repetitious; but the imaginative vision which generated his first three volumes of poetry had been fully expressed in the handful of poems encompassing the Real Me.

Stevens, on the other hand, wrote much of the poetry I have been quoting when he was over sixty years old. He continued to discover the parameters of his own myth throughout his life—largely, one speculates, because the origins of that myth were intellectual and therefore available to revision in the way one's life experiences are not. Stevens, unlike Whitman, worked quite consciously with the analogues between mind and nature which I have been isolating for discussion here. As he wrote to his translator Renato Poggioli, "I want, as poet, to be that in nature which constitutes nature's very self. I want to be nature in the form of a man, with all the resources of nature" (*LWS* 790). Stevens' last poem, found in manuscript after his death, shows that he never exhausted the subject of "nature in the form of a man":

> A mythology reflects its region. Here
> In Connecticut, we never lived in a time
> When mythology was possible. —But if we had—
> That raises the question of the image's truth.
> The image must be of the nature of its creator.
> It is the nature of its creator increased,
> Heightened. It is he, anew in a freshened youth
> And it is he in the substance of his region,
> Wood of his forests and stone out of his fields,
> Or from under his mountains.   [*OP* 118]

Yet Stevens completed his myth only with the volume *The Auroras of Autumn*, where in the title poem, as Harold Bloom has pointed out, Stevens recreates the situation recorded in

Whitman's "As I Ebb'd with the Ocean of Life"[2]–but with a significant difference. Stevens' "Auroras" does not focus, like Whitman's poem, on the fear that the imagination may never again be able to "contain" nature ("Auroras," VI). Rather, there and in the poems following, Stevens explores the implications of another possible meaning of the identification of the imagination with nature, and is able to carry the poet-hero through the period of "total leaflessness" (*CP* 477) and into a new freshening of imaginative life. The last poem in his collection significantly speaks of awakening on a March morning, "at the earliest ending of winter," as to "a new knowledge of reality" (*CP* 534).

This summary may seem to imply that Stevens' late poems were merely "facile exercises" (*CP* 398) on ideas searched out fully in the writing of *Transport to Summer*. But a letter dating from the period of *Auroras* indicates that in 1949 Stevens was still discovering an order rather than imposing one. In a characteristically patient reply to a puzzled graduate student, he wrote:

No, I am not doing a seasonal sequence. It may be that the title of my next book will be The Auroras of Autumn, but this is some little distance ahead and I may not like that title by-and-by as much as I like it now. Nor is there anything autobiographical about it. What underlies this sort of thing is the drift of one's ideas. From the imaginative period of Notes I turned to the ideas of Credences of Summer. At the moment I am at work on a thing called An Ordinary Evening in New Haven . . . here my interest is to try to get as close to the ordinary, the commonplace and ugly as it is possible for a poet to get. It is not a question of grim reality but of plain reality. The object of course is

² Bloom, "The Central Man: Emerson, Whitman, Wallace Stevens," *Massachusetts Review*, VII (Winter 1966), 23ff.

to purge oneself of anything false. I have been doing this since the beginning of March and intend to keep studying the subject and working on it until I am quite through with it. This is not in any sense a turning away from the ideas of Credences of Summer: it is a development of those ideas. That sort of thing might ultimately lead to another phase of what you call a seasonal sequence but certainly it would have nothing to do with the weather: it would have to do with the drift of one's ideas. [*LWS* 636–637]

These remarks about "An Ordinary Evening in New Haven" suggest Stevens' awareness of the degree to which *Transport to Summer* views "plain reality," and even "grim reality," as from under the protection of the imagination's summer. The poems of *Auroras*, on the other hand, probe the states of feeling for which the landscapes of autumn and winter furnish natural metaphors. There is a concentration of poems in the first thirty-five pages ("The Auroras of Autumn" through "Woman in Sunshine") in which an entire seasonal cycle is accomplished. We may here see Stevens' mind in the act of finding and integrating into a mythic whole the elements of what he calls "the unbroken circle of summer" (*CP* 438).

"*The Auroras of Autumn*"

"The Auroras of Autumn" concerns that moment of crisis in the imagination described by W. H. Auden, and is symbolized by Stevens in the figure of the poet in the autumnal phase of imagination as a "scholar of one candle" who opens his door on the lights of the aurora borealis, and feels with fear "an Arctic effulgence flaring on the frame / Of everything he is" (*CP* 417). The poet of autumn, then, is he who has "fallen": away from the imaginative unity with reality "in which majesty is a mirror of the self" (*CP* 405), and into a shocked consciousness of the inhuman majesty of the not-

Me, brilliantly symbolized in the Northern Lights. Harold
Bloom has described this autumnal consciousness as a sense of
"the challenge and fear of a total questioning of the capability
of human imagination to match the power of reality."[3] To
his assessment I would want to add the observation that "reality" in "Auroras" includes not merely nature, but more significantly that which the imagination has added to nature:
the poems—such as "the one about the credible hero" (OP
117)—which stand blazing on the horizon of the poet's achievement and which he may not be able to match. "The Auroras
of Autumn" contemplates the poet's relation to his own poetry, especially the loss of a feeling of repose within "the
central of our being" (CP 380), an experience which, in the
autumnal state, he recalls nostalgically in metaphors of being
at home (in the sections beginning "Farewell to an idea . . .":
II, III, IV). Like the Whitman who muses "late in the autumn
day," Stevens' scholar is accommodated by neither mother
nor father, and is dispossessed even of his own work: the not-
Me is, most poignantly, the heroic poet he was and may
never be again. In order to understand what happens in this
difficult section of the poem, one has to see that part of
Stevens' purpose is to make a Coleridgean distinction between
secondary imagination, the esemplastic power of the mind,
and fancy, "merely circulating" (CP 149). Coleridge's own
definition of these terms is famously unclear, but the difference between them turns on the relevance to each of the ideas
discovered in the acutely perceptive primary phases of the
imagination's cycle. The secondary imagination is the opera-
tive mode of the primary, Coleridge says, "identical with the
primary in the *kind* of its agency, and differing only in *de-*

[3] *Ibid.*, p. 40.

gree, and in the mode of its operation." Fancy, on the other hand, "is indeed no other than a mode of Memory emancipated from the order of time and space"; its movement is arbitrary, and "it must receive all its materials ready made from the law of association" (*Biographia Literaria*, XIII). We can see this same distinction in the two modes of creative activity performed by the giant. In section IV he is addressed as "father" and "Master." As a source of power, the individual poet's potential for writing supreme fictions, he is sought out by the poet in a state of desire for imaginative forms: "What company, / In masks, can choir it with the naked wind?" (*CP* 415). Like the autumn-minded Whitman of "As I Ebb'd with the Ocean of Life," the narrator of "The Auroras of Autumn" is thinking "the old thought of likenesses . . . seeking types" (*LG* 254). He believes in the imagination's power to satisfy his human need—in this case, a poetry adequate to the "great enkindlings" outdoors. But he is offered in the next sections not the poetry of imagination but the poetry of fancy.

Fancy's response to the aurora borealis produces two varieties of poetry. In section V, where memory is the source of images, a colorful mannerism results. The father fetches characters, scenes and costumes from here and there, and assembles them with an eye to grandiose display:

> The father fetches pageants out of air,
> Scenes of the theatre, vistas and blocks of woods
> And curtains like a naive pretence of sleep.
>
> . . . . .
>
> We stand in the tumult of a festival.   [*CP* 415]

The alternative mode of fancy's response to the magnificence of the lights is described in VI, where the law of association, rather than memory, seems to provide the shaping intelligence of a poetry which is like "cloud transformed / To cloud transformed again, idly, the way / A season changes color to no end, / Except the lavishing of itself in change, / . . . because it likes magnificence" (*CP* 415).

Sections V and VI, then, describe an art which is flashy or bold but lacking in ideas, a poetry felt by the narrator to be pretentious and boring. I think it is important to see, however, that Stevens does not reject this poetry simply because it derives from fancy. In Stevens, "flicking from finikin to fine finikin" (*CP* 488) is a delightful employment of the mind, often productive of the most pleasant poetic effects. But in "Auroras" the distinction between imagination and fancy is being made within the framework of feeling and intention focused by the symbol of the lights. The aurora borealis creates throughout the poem the kind of pressure described in "The Noble Rider and the Sound of Words" as the desire for a poetry that is faithful to reality and is also noble: "For the sensitive poet, conscious of negations, nothing is more difficult than the affirmations of nobility and yet there is nothing that he requires of himself more persistently, since in them and in their kind, alone, are to be found those sanctions that are the reasons for his being" (*NA* 35). The auroras represent, among other things, an ultimate threat to the poet's being. But the poem's deep insight is that self-destruction is the necessary other half of self-creation:

The cloud drifts idly through half-thought-of forms.

The theatre is filled with flying birds,
Wild wedges, as of a volcano's smoke, palm-eyed
And vanishing, a web in a corridor

Or massive portico. . . .
· · · · ·

This is nothing until in a single man contained,
Nothing until this named thing nameless is
And is destroyed. He opens the door of his house

On flames.   [*CP* 416–417]

The language here is obscure because of the vagueness of the
demonstrative pronouns. But the next section fills out our
sense of what must be contained and what destroyed. Stevens
returns to the idea of the giant of imagination, whom he had
left sitting motionless (section IV), with a set of questions
that convey a dawning knowledge of the meaning of his own
symbol for the imagination—the "Master" and "father" of section IV—and that, in effect, correct it. In the image of the
giant "seated by the fire / And yet in space and motionless"
depicted in "Auroras," we have had Stevens' version of Whitman's Real Me in "As I Ebb'd": the heroic I, or "man enjoying angels" from *Notes* objectified and addressed as the highest poetic intelligence. The questions that open section VII—
"Is there an imagination that sits enthroned / As grim as it is
benevolent . . . ?" (*CP* 417)—are Stevens' acknowledgment
that the "old intelligence" (*NA* 52) of *Notes* must be destroyed if the narrator would again be poet. The old intelligence has become the intelligence of fancy. Its resources are
not perceptions but memories, the forms it produced in sections V and VI have been self-imitations, parodies. (Section V
seems to be a caricature of the end section of "Credences of
Summer," and VI can be read as a critique of *Harmonium's*
"Sea Surface Full of Clouds.") It must change; Stevens will
now have to imagine in full the nature of the mind that can
say "yes / To no" (*CP* 414). This is what follows the questions in section VII: a giant twice as large, "as grim as it is
benevolent," a symbolic figure who is in every way the negative counterpart to the giant evolved in *Notes toward a Su-*

preme Fiction, but who fulfills the claim made in that poem
that "it must be possible"

> To discover an order as of
> A season, to discover summer and know it,
> To discover winter and know it well.   [*CP* 403–404]

As the arc of summer was in *Transport to Summer* seen as
a finding of form, and repose within the highest day was the
realization of a heroic self within poetic form, so it is seen in
"The Auroras of Autumn" that the arc which completes the
cycle of imagination must be a divesting, an extinguishing,
and that repose within the highest night is total loss of one's
own created images:

> When the leaves are dead
> Does [the imagination] take its place in the north and enfold
>   itself,
> Goat-leaper, crystalled and luminous, sitting
>
> In highest night?
>   . . . . .
> It leaps through us, through all our heavens leaps,
> Extinguishing our planets, one by one,
> Leaving of where we were and looked, of where
>
> We knew each other and of each other thought,
> A shivering residue, chilled and foregone.   [*CP* 417]

This is Stevens' version of Whitman's dark recognition that
the dead leaves that fill his own autumn landscape are

> Me and mine, loose windrows, little corpses,
> Froth, snowy white, and bubbles,
> (See, from my dead lips the ooze exuding at last,
> See, the prismatic colors glistening and rolling)   [*LG* 256]

Whitman takes this recognition of the deadness of his poems
to mean that the Real Me has never really spoken through

him, that "I have not once had the least idea who or what I
am, / . . . I have not really understood any thing, not a single object, and that no man ever can" (*LG* 254). Stevens'
poem appears to originate also in radical mistrust of his own
poetic metaphors ("We stand in the tumult of a festival. /
What festival? This loud disordered mooch?" [*CP* 415]).
But Stevens' mood in contemplating this subject is characteristically more analytical than Whitman's. Stevens conceives
such "death" to be a necessary stage in the continuing life of
the mind, and not only that, but a state which must be *willed*
by the poet who has achieved a heroic voice and seeks to
write another poem which is noble and yet is true to things
as they are. In the final stanzas of this section he recognizes
that grim imagination as not alien, mystic, or divine, but accessible to the will:

> it dare not leap by chance in its own dark.
> It must change from destiny to slight caprice.
> And thus its jetted tragedy, its stele
>
> And shape and mournful making move to find
> What must unmake it and, at last, what can.   [*CP* 417–418]

In the figure of the giant who must seek to unmake himself
we have the last character in Stevens' mythology of imagination: the personification of the phase in which "it dissolves,
diffuses, dissipates in order to recreate." Stevens' reader has
encountered aspects of this persona before, notably in the
mock-hero Crispin, and in the description of the mind of winter which "lashes more fiercely than the wind, / As the mind,
to find what will suffice, destroys / Romantic tenements of
rose and ice" (*CP* 239). But in "The Auroras of Autumn"
what were before merely parts of a world are united by a
poetic intelligence which, like Yeats's, seems to have strength-
ened and grown more capable of synthesis as it aged. The

name of Yeats is relevant here, for "Auroras" can be read as
Stevens' meditation on the theme of "The Circus Animals'
Desertion," and for all its difficulties, Stevens' is the more sat-
isfying poem. The rhetorical form of Yeats' poem involves at
its opening a statement of contempt for his own completed
work—a contempt softened in the thoughtfulness of the second section, and retracted at the end of the poem with Yeats's
choice again to "lie down where all the ladders start." The
feeling in Stevens' poem is more complicated and, one judges,
more true. "Auroras" is deeply nostalgic, full of the knowledge that "Only the half we can never possess remains" (*CP*
413). Yet Stevens is even more tough-minded than Yeats in
his understanding that to find "the Mother's face, the purpose of the poem" (*CP* 413) means first to find the serpent
whose nest is in the Northern Lights (section I). Stevens conceives this process as going back not to a place—the childhood
home or Yeats's "heart"—but to an *idea*, "a thing of ether that
exists almost as predicate" (section VIII). The way to the
idea is destruction of the completed heroic imagination, via
the unimpeded activity of the grim giant. Translated, I think
we can take Stevens' last words in section VII—

> [Its] shape and mournful making move to find
> What must unmake it and, at last, what can,
> Say, a flippant communication under the moon

—to mean that the poet must be willing, like Yeats, to turn the
sharpest, most ironic edges of his mind against his beloved
creations, and to make this a creative act, part of the effort on
the one hand to "purge oneself of anything false," and on the
other, to avoid "mere repetitions." This knowledge is the wisdom of the serpent in the poem, "flashing to wished-for dis-
appearances." By a process of denying his own completed im-

ages, Stevens will disown the rich, communal, heroic world of *Transport to Summer*. He will suffer, too, in the stripping away. The autumn of the mind is a hard time for the poet; it feels to Stevens, as to Whitman, like oncoming death, a death symbolized by both poets in terms of dead leaves, sticks, corpses:

> Shall we be found hanging in the trees next spring?
> Of what disaster is this the imminence:
> Bare limbs, bare trees and a wind as sharp as salt?   [*CP* 419]

But "Farewell to an idea" involves a "clearing of sight," or a return to the phase of the primary imagination, "the living power and prime agent of all human Perception and . . . a repetition in the finite mind of the eternal act of creation in the infinite I AM." In Stevens the religious rhetoric is refracted through a qualifying irony insisting that the infinite is that which changes. But the religious meaning is not denied. If experience at the pole of winter—"Inhalations of original cold / And of original earliness" (*CP* 481)—is described by Stevens as "a daily sense, / Not the predicate of bright origin" (*CP* 481), it is nonetheless the rediscovery of innocence, a rebirth of the spirit. We are told this in "Auroras," VIII, to which we may return.

The scholar has, in the course of "Auroras," stepped "barefoot into reality" (*CP* 423). He has opened the door of his shelter and allowed the serpentine lights to possess his being, has seen the "Arctic effulgence flaring on the frame / Of everything he is." The lights "fill the being before the mind can think" (*CP* 436), for this is the phase of primary imagination. But thought follows. Section VIII suggests that the instant in which self was lost in the lights was the finding also of the serpent, "the bodiless," and that having been confronted, he disappears. Evil vanishes and innocence is disclosed in its

place. The Northern Lights are not a serpent: they simply
are.

> So, then, these lights are not a spell of light,
> A saying out of a cloud, but innocence.
> An innocence of the earth and no false sign
>
> Or symbol of malice. That we partake thereof,
> Lie down like children in this holiness,
> As if, awake, we lay in the quiet of sleep,
>
> As if the innocent mother sang in the dark
> Of the room and on an accordian, half-heard,
> Created the time and place in which we breathed.   [*CP* 419]

Stevens is here describing a change in the mind's orientation
to its object. Relinquishing fear-shadowed interpretations of
the significance of the Not-Me, the mind discovers that "The
actual is a deft beneficence" (*CP* 155), "Reality is the beginning not the end" (*CP* 469). Then a surge of grateful love,
released by this perception, shapes the metaphorical "as ifs"
that carry the section to its conclusion. For this moment of
primary imagination, when "sense lies still, as a man lies, /
Enormous, in a completing of his truth" (*CP* 431), is the moment of the poet's union with his muse. It restores him to a
creative cycle of the mind which, like the creative cycle of
the year, can carry him to the heroic "abundance of being"
(*CP* 445) which is its fortune.

This last intuition, however, remains outside the experience
of the poem, for the completed cycle is viewed in "Auroras"
wholly through the sensibility of the troubled mind of autumn, the poet's bad time. "It may come tomorrow in the
simplest word" (*CP* 420), but for the present he has only his
intellectual hope and the gathering dark. The remainder of
the poems in the volume *The Auroras of Autumn*, however,

strengthen into assertion what is only projected as possible here—exploring the idea of "the unbroken circle of summer" (*CP* 438) with a refreshed certainty of its truth as metaphor. The ice shadow of the sky is seen, a few pages further on, to be "Blue for all that / . . . with water running in the sun" (*CP* 438); February becomes the month of "the imagination's mercies / . . . Something returning from a deeper quarter, / A glacier running through delirium" (*CP* 439).

"*The Rock*"

"The Auroras of Autumn," however, is only a next-to-last poem concerning heroic consciousness. Stevens' "last" poem about the hero is "The Rock." Though no less affirmative of the mind's regenerative powers, "The Rock" takes into greater account the darkness that precedes the light in the mind of "Auroras."

"The Rock" absorbs the fact of mortality into the myth of the heroic self completed in "Auroras." "The Rock" contemplates the meaning of the past. The unarticulated question it seeks to answer is a question of final belief: how can a man achieve a sense of the continuity of his own life, and belief in its meaning, if the way to possession of the present is through what Stevens has called "forgetfulness"?

The answer is made in three parts. "Seventy Years Later" rejects memory as a source of confirmation that we were ever alive. The poem has a complicated argument, for Stevens wants to insist that the experience of "the meeting at noon at the edge of a field" with his green and fluent mundo *was* "an incessant being alive"; but at the same time to insist that *recall* of that experience is an encounter with shadows, not the discovery of an object of belief. The same is true of all recall,

even of the childhood home, or of the sounds of the blue
guitar: "The lives these lived in the mind are at an end" (*CP*
525). His subtle point, however, is that the experience recalled
was itself produced by something in the mind, a "theorem"
proposed between self and the world by a self desperately in
need of belief: the theorem that nothingness contained in its
permanent cold "a possibleness." And this was

an illusion so desired

> That the green leaves came and covered the high rock,
> That the lilacs came and bloomed, like a blindness cleaned,
> Exclaiming bright sight, as it was satisfied.   [*CP* 526]

These lilacs and green leaves are of course not real, but fictions—like Whitman's "scented herbage of my breast" (*LG*
113). In the next part, "The Poem as Icon" (*CP* 626), Stevens deals with the question of whether the mind faithful to
reality will have to reject its fictions, like its memories, as
illusions. Stevens argues it will not. He proposes that the
leaves may be regarded as credible objects of belief—"icons"—
because they did not wither after a while, but rather grew:
broke into bud, broke into bloom, and bore fruit; and because
the poet who ate of their culls found that the ground of human being analogous to rock—"the gray particular of man's
life" (*CP* 528)—had been cured. The fiction of the leaves
thus becomes "the figuration of blessedness." It is a witty reversal of the myth of Adam's Fall, but the wit is submerged
in the deep joy the discovery opens on. The fiction of the
leaves is, of course, the idea that the human mind is a tree
which buds and blooms and bears fruit "without change,"
though the fruits themselves fall to cure and nourish other
men. As long as the man continues to love the earth, to root
his mind in it, so long does the fruit abundantly come, and

In this plenty, the poem makes meanings of the rock,
Of such mixed motion and such imagery
That its barrenness becomes a thousand things

And so exists no more. This is the cure
Of leaves and of the ground and of ourselves.   [CP 527]

This is a cure beyond "forgetfulness" because it testifies to continuity: the poet's continuity with other men and with his own past as well. For he can see that his earliest thought has produced his present understanding, just as seeds annually shed produce the next season's fruit. All the poems collected into Stevens' big book, from the earliest gathered into *Harmonium* through the latest written for *The Rock*, furnish their parts toward the icon of the man who speaks to us in these pages. They began in love of the earth and flourished in faithfulness to her. Stevens, like God on the sixth day when he created man in his own image, looks on his creation and finds it good.

The last part, "Forms of the Rock in a Night Hymn," completes the intelligence that the mind is of earth, and that "there is nothing else." Here Stevens speaks of the "difficulty of what it is to be," because while the rock is the "stone from which [man] rises up," (*CP* 528) it is equally—and at last— "the step to the bleaker depths of his descents." In this poem the poet stands looking into night and, acknowledging that the mind is an enclosed space, not infinite, attempts to comprehend the "difficult rightness" of what it sees. Mortality is, of course, one of the things implied. Tranquility comes with comprehension. The syntax is very difficult. The poem moves with a logic of feeling, in which the need for precise expression—a need conveyed in the pedantic rhetoric typical of Stevens in one mood (lines 1–13)—gradually falls away. By the last lines grammatical coherence has completely disappeared

and the gazing mind seems simply transfixed by what it perceives. This is primary imagination:

> It is the rock where tranquil must adduce
> Its tranquil self, the main of things, the mind,
>
> The starting point of the human and the end,
> That in which space itself is contained, the gate
> To the enclosure, day, the things illumined
>
> By day, night, and that which night illumines,
> Night and its midnight-minting fragrances,
> Night's hymn of the rock, as in a vivid sleep.   [CP 528]

Stevens ends "The Rock" with words like organ-sounds saying "yes / To no; and in saying yes he says farewell" (CP
414).

   This thought brings us back to "The Auroras of Autumn,"
the poem which I think can be said to have made "The Rock"
possible. As I mentioned above, the regeneration of the poetic
self, though confirmed in every section of "Auroras," does
not take place within the dramatic and psychological situation explored in the poem. Yet reasons accounting for Stevens' further development as a poet may be located in it, as
reasons why Whitman relinquished the persona of the Real
Me after 1860 can be located in "As I Ebb'd with the Ocean
of Life." These remarks do not preface a judgment that Stevens is the better poet. I hope we shall never know which to
prefer: the beauty of inflections or the beauty of innuendoes.
But if the critic's purpose is to locate and describe the things
that seem to make all the difference, we may return for a last
look at "The Auroras of Autumn" and "As I Ebb'd with the
Ocean of Life," the poems in which each writer records his
fear he may never write authentically again.

   Each poem moves to closure as the narrator lies down like
a child in a place made sacred by understanding, submitting

to authority. For Whitman this submission involved flinging himself prostrate on Paumanok, site of his original discovery of the potentially heroic self within him, the discovery recounted in "Out of the Cradle Endlessly Rocking." The gesture prefaces his acknowledgment, in the last section of "As I Ebb'd with the Ocean of Life," that his personal experiences, resources of the poetry of the Real Me, have been produced, like the phenomenal world itself, out of some unending natural process of which destruction is an aspect now come, without his will or understanding, to himself:

> [I have been] buoy'd hither from many moods, one contradicting another,
> From the storm, the long calm, the darkness, the swell,
> Musing, pondering, a breath, a briny tear, a dab of liquid or soil,
> Up just as much from fathomless workings fermented and thrown.   [LG 256]

Whitman courageously accepts the authority of unfathomable Nature even if it means destruction of the consciousness of the Real Me. "I mean tenderly by you and all," he says to his threatening parents, "oceans both" (LG 255). From our advantageous perspective in time we can find prophetic irony in the fact that his poem ends with the narrator lying in drifts at our feet. Whitman had, up to that time, placed his whole faith in his personal biography as the source of "hints" or analogues for poems, and there is evidence that at the period of the composition of "As I Ebb'd with the Ocean of Life" he was suffering from traumatic self-revulsion, having discovered himself to be homosexual—a situation for which the male "soul" is a comprehensible, if unconscious, symbol. Whitman's profound belief in the authority of his own experience faltered after 1861, and with it vanished the persona of the

Real Me as speaker of the authentic lines. From then on Whitman is the poet of democracy or of the mystic "aggregate" ("Eidolons"): in either case, of a myth in which Self merges with Other in a process that refuses to investigate distinctions.

The end of "Auroras" recomposes the situation Whitman depicts in "As I Ebb'd with the Ocean of Life." But for Wallace Stevens the sacred place has no spatial location: "There may be always a time of innocence. / There is never a place" (*CP* 418). Innocence, the condition of primary imagination, is a state of mind. In the autumn of the creative cycle, it is a change of mind, the relinquishing of an exhausted mode of thought. Yet,

> If it is not a thing of time, nor of place,
>
> Existing in the idea of it, alone,
> In the sense against calamity, it is not
> Less real.
>   . . . . .
> Like a book at evening beautiful but untrue,
> Like a book on rising beautiful and true.   [*CP* 418]

In a psychological act analogous to Whitman's act of flinging himself prostrate, Stevens gives up the effort of mind which has been pressing, throughout his meditation, back against the pressure of the reality symbolized by the auroras. Purged of memory and desire, purged of fear, he settles down to listen again to a fatherly voice that can "Breathe . . . the secret of the murmuring I envy" (*LG* 255):

> An unhappy people in a happy world—
> Read, rabbi, the phases of this difference.
>   . . . . .
> Read to the congregation, for today
> And for tomorrow, this extremity,
> This contrivance of the spectre of the spheres,

Contriving balance to contrive a whole,
The vital, the never-failing genius,
Fulfilling his meditations, great and small.   [*CP* 420]

The rabbi will know which pages to read the diminished man, since he is a scholar of texts containing the fulfilled meditations of the central man—texts called by Stevens in this same volume, "purple tabulae, / The outlines of being and its expressings, the syllables of its law: / *Poesis* . . ." ("Large Red Man Reading" [*CP* 423]).

Comparing the closures of these two dejection odes, one can observe that where Whitman addresses a mystical Father as the potential source of enlightenment, Stevens consults tradition, "*poesis*, the literal characters, the vatic lines." It may be objected that Stevens' resolution of the crisis Whitman treats in moving emotional terms is too intellectual. Yet Whitman was forty when he wrote "A I Ebb'd," a man in the prime of life who had suddenly come to doubt whether his vocation was, in any important sense, work: "I perceive I have not really understood any thing, not a single object, and that no man ever can" (*LG* 254). Stevens at sixty-eight is beyond this doubt, and his affirmations of imagination as value in the poems of *The Auroras of Autumn* and *The Rock* are profoundly personal. Yet they are not merely affirmations of his own creative energy late in life. Rather, the poems of these volumes convey the state of mind that Erik Erikson describes as "ego integrity," the final stage of maturity in the human psyche:

Lacking a clear definition, I shall point to a few constituents of this state of mind. It is the ego's accrued assurance of its proclivity for order and meaning. It is a post-narcissistic love of the human ego—not of the self—as an experience which conveys some world order and spiritual sense, no matter how dearly paid for . . . for [the possessor of integrity] all human integrity stands or falls with the one style of integrity of which he partakes. The style of integrity developed by his culture or civilization thus becomes the "patrimony of his soul," the seal of his moral paternity of himself. . . . In such final consolidation, death loses its sting.[4]

I think this is the aspiration to centrality we see developed in Stevens' *Collected Poems*, based on a difficult self-acceptance from which the merely accidental dimensions of personality have been withheld as irrelevant, so that what we are given is a mythic form, an object of belief.

> The fiction of the leaves is the icon
>
> Of the poem, the figuration of blessedness,
> And the icon is the man.   [*CP* 526]

Whether Stevens thought he had achieved a degree of spiritual centrality within American culture—the kind of centrality Whitman knew he had achieved in "Song of Myself"—is hard to gauge. In one of the last of his poems he suggests not:

> The master of the spruce, himself,
> Became transformed. But his mastery
>
> Left only the fragments found in the grass,
> From his project, as finally magnified.   [*CP* 515]

But we are speaking of the iconic self, the only one who remains of either poet. And the reader who turns to Whitman or Stevens again and again seeking "the vivid transparence that you bring" could say of both books what Whitman said of his own: Who touches this touches a man.

---

[4] Erikson, *Childhood and Society*, p. 268.

Index of Stevens' Works

233

Index of Whitman's Works

General Index

Walt Whitman and Wallace Stevens

Designed by R. E. Rosenbaum.
Composed by York Composition Co., Inc.
in 11 point linotype Janson, 3 points leaded,
with display lines in Weiss.
Printed letterpress from type by York Composition Co., Inc.
on Warren's No. 66 text, 50 pound basis,
with the Cornell University Press watermark.
Bound by Vail-Ballou Press.